FACING REDU

Surviving and

FACING REDUNDANCY

Surviving and Thriving

Jenny Rogers

McGraw-Hill Education
McGraw-Hill House
Shoppenhangers Road
Maidenhead
Berkshire
England
SL6 2QL

Website: www.mcgraw-hill.co.uk

and Two Penn Plaza, New York, NY 10121–2289, USA

First published 2014

A catalogue record of this book is available from the British Library

ISBN-13: 978-0-07-715828-6 (pb)
ISBN-10: 0-07-71828-8 (pb)
eISBN: 978-0-07-715829-3

Library of Congress Cataloging-in-Publication Data
CIP data applied for

Typesetting and e-book compilations by
RefineCatch Limited, Bungay, Suffolk

Praise for this book

"Rogers' Facing Redundancy *brings a deep level of honesty, insight, and most importantly practical support, for career transition in the 21st century"*

Katherine Tulpa, CEO, Association for Coaching

"This is a stunning book: easy to read, very informative, packed full of common-sense good advice derived from years of experience. The case studies are short and interesting. It's not an exaggeration to say I couldn't put it down. Highly recommended."

Carolyn Gray, Group Director, HR, Pensions & Sustainability, Guardian Media Group

CONTENTS

Foreword ix

About the author xi

Acknowledgements xii

Introduction xiv

Ten top tips for managing redundancy

1 **The shock** 1

Why redundancy hurts and how to shorten the time to adjustment

2 **Emergency advice** 23

How and why it is so important to protect your reputation and well-being during the immediate process of being given the news. How to exit with grace

3 **Getting help** 47

Finding a range of helpers and getting the most out of them

4 **How did this happen?** 69

Understanding why redundancy has happened, including what individuals may have contributed

5 **Follow the money** 85

Working out where your money is going; implementing a 'Scrimper's Charter'

6 **What you want, what you offer** 105

Why it matters to see yourself as a brand. Assessing your whole life not just work, identifying what a dream job would look like

7 Thinking beyond your taken-for-granteds 127

The importance of not getting stuck on fixed ideas about your next job. Where and how you might compromise

8 Job search: what really works 141

Getting past unhelpful myths about job search. How to understand and exploit the informal jobs market; using social media

9 Powerful CVs 161

The role of a CV in job search. How to construct a CV that has impact

10 Secrets of success at the interview 175

Demystifying the job interview; understanding the process from the employer's perspective; managing nervousness; preparation that counts

11 The alternative life 191

Exploring new types of career and life: freelance, interim and portfolio working

Index 211

FOREWORD

Cary L. Cooper

We are living in turbulent economic times, and for many people who suffer the indignity and feelings of rejection by being made redundant, they may experience hopelessness and a fear of the future, let alone a worry about their financial security (Weinberg & Cooper, 2012). As Machiavelli wrote in a different 16th Century world in The Prince, in the face of great change "many people have believed and still do believe. . . .they can't do anything about it and have no way of protecting themselves. As a result they may decide it's hardly worth making an effort and just leave events to chance" (Parks, 2009). Given the scale of job loss in Europe over the last seven years, with very high levels of unemployment not seen since the 1930s, and with youth unemployment ranging from 25 to over 50% in many EU countries, 'resilience' has got to be the watchword of the future. We need to encourage people who lose their job to take control, to see that there are opportunities out there, which may be better and more rewarding than what they did in the past.

Although being made redundant is an emotionally rejecting event, it can also be one in which the individual can use it to consider a range of options in life, to find another path to a more fulfilling work life, getting greater balance and having more control, in essence, enjoying greater job satisfaction and meaning from work. As Leonardo da Vinci once wrote "every now and then go away and have a little relaxation. To remain constantly at work will diminish your judgement. Go some distance away, because work will be in perspective and a lack of harmony is more readily seen". Working in the same job for many years can have this effect, and although losing a job is very stressful, it can also be an opportunity to think of new challenges.

The author of this book offers practical ways to help those who have been made redundant to answer some of the following questions: "how do I keep my dignity and self-esteem through the process of being made redundant, and get the best deal I can?" and "what is the best way of seizing the opportunity to redesign my life and career?". Being positive and taking control are the answers to dealing with redundancy, and this book has plenty of energising tips on how to do this. This is the beginning of the process of change, as Mark Twain once quipped "If you always do what you always did, you'll always get what you always got!"

References:

Parks,T. (2009) The Prince by Niccolo Machiavelli. London: Penguin.

Weinberg, A. & Cooper, C.L. (2012) Stress in Turbulent Times. Basingstoke: Palgrave Macmillan.

Cary L. Cooper, CBE, is Distinguished Professor of Organizational Psychology and Health, Lancaster University Management School, UK

ABOUT THE AUTHOR

Jenny Rogers is one of the UK's most experienced coaches. Her clients include chief executives in central and local government, banking and finance, professional service organizations, ambassadors, senior scientists, senior executives in the BBC and other broadcasting organizations, the arts and marketing. She also works with people in middle- and junior-level jobs who face career challenges. She has successfully coached many hundreds of people through career crises. She has published books on how to create a powerful CV and how to be successful at a job interview and has been a frequent contributor to BBC Radio.

As well as running her own coaching practice, Jenny teaches and trains coaches internationally. She is a full member of APECS, the UK accrediting body for senior coaches.

www.jennyrogerscoaching.com

Twitter: @jennyrogers10

ACKNOWLEDGEMENTS

To my clients: I'm well aware that you take a chance in trusting a stranger with what are often difficult emotions and major life-questions. Thank you for taking that risk and, going back to my earliest days as a coach more than 22 years ago, for letting me practise on you and for appearing to forgive the mistakes that even the most experienced coach will make from time to time. Some of you have become dear friends: you know who you are. This means I cannot be your coach but the friendship is even more enjoyable.

To other thinkers in this field such as John Lees and James Innes: thank you for doing so much of the thinking and for keeping pegging away at career coaching topics – for too long the Cinderella of coaching. Special thanks to Richard Bolles whose magnificent book *What Color is Your Parachute?* is a wonderful resource and a good example of how knowing your life purpose shapes and simplifies everything you do. Thanks too to The Coaches Training Institute in California for being the first to synthesize so many ideas about coaching itself. Your book *Co-Active Coaching* inspired me and many others to become full-time coaches. And thanks to all those distinguished social psychologists such as Michael Argyle whose student I was while doing a post-graduate Diploma at Oxford in the Sixties and who first alerted me to the intriguing and infuriating nature of human perception and psychology.

To friends and colleagues: many of you have been through the ordeal of redundancy and have come out smiling. Your stories, your courage and your willingness to share a lot of this with me inspired me to write this book. Special thanks to those who have given me so much good company, good advice, good wine, good listening – sometimes through dark times: David Harding and Chris Longley, Kim Lavely and Magee, Vince and Wendi Dallanegra, Leni Wildflower and Joe Treasure.

To my Commissioning Editor, Monika Lee: a wise, steady, encouraging presence – always.

To my PA, Angela Adams: we have worked together for 18 years and you are still patient with my diary bodge-ups, my inability to understand VAT and general hopelessness with anything practical. Thank you for knowing how to do all of those things.

To my family: I know you think it bizarre that I claim to find it relaxing to write books when we are all on holiday but you're used to it now and even make the odd encouraging comment. Thank you for your tolerance. And a remembrance for my dear husband Alan who relentlessly encouraged people in their careers, believed in their strengths, including mine, and gave many now well-known broadcasters their first chance when no one else would.

To my cat, Freddy: good cat. I forgive you for your obsession with sitting on the keyboard while I type.

I am interested in your comments on this book: all feedback is welcome including ideas on how it might be improved in any subsequent edition. Please email me: Jenny@JennyRogersCoaching.com. My website address is www.JennyRogersCoaching.com.

INTRODUCTION

Losing your job is one of the most difficult of life's challenges. In the negative impact it can have, it's right up there with divorce, managing a big debt, bereavement and serious illnesses. As with all these other challenges, it is frequently the case that such troubles do not come singly. Losing your job may expose weaknesses in other aspects of your life, which is why being made redundant may be followed by cracks in relationships, or by illness and money problems.

This sounds grim, yet even at the height of recession, in my own work as a coach almost all of the many people who have come to me for help with this crisis have been able to move on. This book is about how to make the transition as short and easy as possible. From now on your job is to find a new job and to design a new life for yourself. It's about taking control and making conscious choices, moving from 'this happened to me' to 'I can make things happen that suit me'.

The book represents what I have learnt from my clients. Through them I have seen at first hand what works and what doesn't. Everything in it is common sense and much of it widely known, yet employers continue to tell me that candidates don't prepare effectively for interviews, and recruiters will describe desperate people wasting time on job search techniques that don't work and never have. Myths about finding a job are still widespread: for instance that it is a good idea to spray your CV out by the hundred, that it's sensible to go for an interview 'just for the practice', that the best way to find a job is to reply to an online advertisement, that in order to find a new job you will have to undertake extensive retraining or that you have to be boastful and aggressive. None of this is true.

Perhaps it is not too surprising that the unhelpful ideas persist. Many people can reach their forties or older without ever having had to construct a CV; in long-stay organizations, much recruiting and selecting has been done informally, so the process of searching for a job elsewhere is a mystery, made worse by the suspicion that maybe your skills are not transferable, though usually they are. The good news here is that even when you are starting as a complete beginner in job search, none of it is difficult and all of it can be learnt and applied immediately.

Ten top tips for managing redundancy

There is much more about all of these themes later in the book, but here are my ten top tips for managing yourself through redundancy:

1. Keep up a cheerful, calm public face. It never pays to gripe bitterly about the employer's sins and failings, however justified you feel you are in naming them. The person who will suffer is you. Avoid all the common traps of expressing anger, hurt – or just slinking away. Make sure you exit from your previous organization with aplomb.
2. Assemble an inner group of helpers, people who are on your side and can offer support, challenge and expert advice. Take full advantage of any offers of help whether from recruiters, legal advisers, workshops, outplacement experts, counsellors or coaches.
3. The more you can get involved and take control of the process, the quicker you will feel better and the easier the transition will be.
4. Get a grip on your finances. Many people are not clear about their commitments and spending patterns. You may

have to economize while you are looking for a new job, but the only sensible way to do this is by starting with a careful analysis of your current spending.

5. A job does not define you: however much you like your work, it is only one part of who you are; use the experience to weigh up what you want from work – and from life. Unwelcome though redundancy usually is, it can be an opportunity to reassess your priorities.
6. See yourself as a brand looking for a buyer. Do what all successful brands do – differentiate yourself. This applies to every aspect of job-searching from how you construct your CV to how you dress to how you behave in an interview.
7. The informal jobs market is a better source of potential jobs than waiting to see what is advertised. Map your network to see who you know and then get your network to help you, through as many different approaches as possible, using the 'generous networking' principle of giving help as often as you ask for it.
8. Develop a strategic plan for your job search, using every available route including social media and personal contacts.
9. Be prepared to move and to abandon declining sectors. There is still plenty of work, and many businesses are thriving despite recession. Be realistic about salary. Don't get hung up on fancy job titles or on exceeding what you were paid in your last job. Sometimes it is better to have a job at all than to be unemployed. Once you are in a new job you can often negotiate salary increases and use the new job as a platform to the next.
10. The employment market is changing rapidly and more people are now discovering the pleasures of working for themselves or of combining part-time jobs. Depending on what else is going on in your life, consider designing a portfolio career: for instance, a mix of freelance, part-time and volunteer work.

The case studies

Confidentiality is a serious promise from coach to client, but a book like this needs examples from experience to bring the principles alive. The dozens of brief case studies in this book have been developed in two ways. First, they have come from accounts written directly by my clients, where they have chosen their own camouflage. Secondly, I have blended three or more real-life stories, with additional disguises, to make a particular point. However, although these are carefully fictionalized, the feelings and principles they illustrate are 100% authentic.

The new world of employment

From having been a rare event, shrouded in shame, being made redundant is now common. It could happen to you more than once. The secret is to see every job, however permanent it claims to be, as a short-term assignment, a project which is about your own learning and development and one that will be followed by another project, probably in a different organization and needing different skills. While in a job, however pleasant, it is sensible to be thinking about your exit and getting ready for the next one, making sure that you are continuously assessing how your own needs are changing, what the employment market needs and developing new skills. The days of an unbroken career with a comfortable pension at the end of it are over. Most of us will change careers at least three times and will continue to work well past what used to be considered retirement age.

It is also true that for some people it is desperately difficult to find a job. If you live in an area of very high unemployment, have few marketable skills, a disability or a patchy employment record, the few jobs that there are will probably be snapped up by people who are overqualified for them and it will be far harder to find work.

What this means is that you have to understand and work the jobs market, viewing yourself as the product and forgetting any idea that employers can see for themselves that you have a solid track record, that you are a decent person and that they should hire you. You have to attract them, not wait for them to attract you. You have to look at any job for what it is: a source of pleasure and learning in the here and now, not some kind of investment that will produce reward in the distant future. You are in charge of your own career, and how you take it forward is in your own hands. The rest of this book is about how to do this in a way that is enjoyable and that lands you a good job and a better life.

1 THE SHOCK

Redundancy hurts. The very word is unpleasant: redundant – no longer needed, surplus to requirements, obsolete. It's no good people telling you soothingly that it's the job that has been made redundant, not you. It feels exactly as if you have been personally singled out to be told that you, the intrinsic person, have been labelled useless.

Zach worked on the IT helpdesk of a consultancy. His job, along with those of his colleagues, was outsourced to one of the giant companies now providing so much of what used to be small, local and in house. He says, 'They alleged it was all about cost and efficiency, but I couldn't see that. All I could see was that eight years of my hard work had been pronounced pointless and me along with it'.

Shelley specialized in courses for people in their first line management role. Her employer decided that there would be a 'rationalization' where several regional training departments would be combined. Shelley did not get one of the jobs in the new department because the focus was to be on provision for more senior managers. In describing this, Shelley's comment was, 'I was getting rave reviews from participants on courses. But this counted for nothing. I felt I'd been swept aside and that no one in senior management had ever really cared one way or the other about the quality of what I did. It was unbelievably hurtful'.

Even when people have volunteered for redundancy, it can still feel difficult to manage:

> *Yes, I was a volunteer but when I got the letter the words looked so bleak – had I made the right decision? Was I giving up security for the unknown?*

Why does it hurt so much?

Research into how our brains work is beginning to explain how we process emotional shocks. There is biology as well as psychology at work here. Just above the human brainstem there are two pea-sized parts of the brain called the amygdala. They are the brain's sentry system, constantly on the alert for danger. They send a flood of the hormone cortisol to the pre-frontal cortex, the part of the brain that is responsible for thinking and strategy, shutting down much of its operation by depriving it of oxygen and glucose. This is because, faced with physical danger, our early ancestors needed oxygen and glucose sent to their muscles in order to run away fast. Our brains and bodies are essentially the same as in those early days. Being told that your job is about to disappear feels like an attack, not a physical but a psychological attack and the brain reacts in the identical way that it did when we were an emerging species 150,000 years ago on the African savannah and faced with a human or animal enemy.

People who have been through redundancy are often stunned later to realize how emotional their immediate responses were:

> *Couldn't think. Couldn't talk. Traumatized, stunned, silent.*
>
> *Felt tearful all the time. Someone who was sympathetic, which lots of people were, would send me into a fit of crying all over again. Who was this crying person? I seemed so unlike my normal self.*
>
> *Angry – angry at my boss, angry with colleagues who still had jobs, angry at the organization for not averting something that could have been averted.*

We pride ourselves on our ability to think. In fact we call our own species *Homo sapiens*, wise man. So how is it that we respond to a crisis like redundancy in what may later seem like an unwise or childlike way? The answer is that although indeed we have *consciousness*, in other words the ability, unlike other

mammals to think about thinking, to strategize, to remember the past and imagine the future, we are in thrall to the emotional centre of the brain, the limbic system. This has far more power over us than most people realize. If you think now about any major decision you have made in your life – for instance whether to live with a new partner, have a child, buy a house – for certain you will find that this decision will have been made on emotional grounds and only later justified with rationality. This is normal; it is what virtually everyone experiences and is nothing to be ashamed of. The task is always to shorten the period where emotion dominates, but you cannot bypass it altogether.

Five human needs

Redundancy has the power to trigger emotional responses in five areas that brain research shows human beings care about a lot. We have basic survival needs that are as much concerned with emotional as physical survival, and the brain networks involved seem to be the same. Also it seems that our brains are more finely tuned to see threat than to see reward and that the need to protect ourselves from threat is never far from our minds, though probably not at a conscious level. Researchers like the writer David Rock in his book *Coaching with the Brain in Mind* (Wiley, 2009) have classified these needs using the acronym SCARF which stands for status, certainty, autonomy, relatedness and fairness. All are intricately involved in the experience of redundancy.

Status

Paid work confers status. You are getting real money for your labour and therefore you perceive yourself as having value. It feels like an affront to status to lose a job. Even where you still have a job because something else is found for you, there can be hurt and indignation when change means an existing post is made redundant.

The hospital decided it couldn't afford care for its own staff which is weird in itself, so my job as a senior physio in Occupational Health was made redundant. I went back to being an ordinary physio and the person I'd been managing became my boss. It was humiliating and it has left me permanently restless and unsettled.

Dot was a messenger in a big civil service department, work that she found intensely enjoyable. 'I delivered parcels, confidential papers, escorted visitors, anything really, and often met famous politicians. I felt I was doing something that mattered. I liked walking down Whitehall every day and I felt proud of my uniform.' Email and the internet diminished the need for her role and at the age of 58, only a few years short of retirement age, she was made redundant. 'I felt upset even though I could see why they'd made the decision. I got a job in a shop but it wasn't the same. Saying, *Oh yes, I'm a sales assistant* isn't like saying *I work for the government*.'

The more senior you are, the more likely this is to be part of your response. Human beings are hierarchical creatures. A wise boss can distinguish between position power – the authority conferred by your role – and moral power, the authority that comes from who you are and how you behave, irrespective of your formal position. But it is all too easy to be deceived into believing that people are behaving warmly and respectfully towards you because they like and honour you as a person.

Bernard was a chief executive in the NHS. As a result of a merger his job disappeared and he had already decided not to compete for the chief executive role in the new organization. He was surprised and hurt to find that this instantly

seemed to change all the relationships around him. 'The news of my impending departure spread quickly. But I still had to attend meetings while the merger was being negotiated. I found that people I had considered to be my peers, other chief execs and directors, who had previously been friendly and attentive, tended to turn away when I came into the room. I found it much harder to make my points in the meetings: I felt I was being brushed off. I felt invisible. In the office I'd ask for things to be done – and often they weren't. No one was outright rude, but the change was palpable.'

Certainty

The human brain likes certainty. Even when we are miserable about our current circumstances, it can feel safer to stay with the status quo than to make a major change. Redundancy removes the certainty of a familiar daily routine and this can be as much about the small things – the journey to work, the latte you take in with you in the morning – to the big things, the salary at the end of the month, the effects on relationships and everyday living. What will I do to fill my time? Will I be able to pay my mortgage? How will my family respond to the loss of my job?

> *I realized that the pay-off would allow me to live OK – if I was careful – for about a year; no holidays, sell the car, cut down on expensive eating out and so on. But in the middle of the night I'd often wake up in a cold sweat thinking, what if I don't get another job ever? Will I have to sell my flat? Should I move out of Edinburgh now? If that happened, how would I cope without all my friends?*

Uncertainty can be hard to live with, but one of the secrets of surviving redundancy is to concentrate on what is actually certain and there may be more of this than you realize at first: family support, a little more financial security than you are acknowledging, loyal friends – and so on.

It can also help to speak your ultimate worries aloud. There is a difference here between plausible and implausible worries. Worrying can seem as if it is a useful activity, but it is only useful if it results in the realization that there is something you can do to tackle the worry straight away. For instance, it is plausible to worry about your finances and this is why it helps to sit down and work out carefully what your actual costs and commitments are. (There is more about this in Chapter 5.) It is not plausible to ask yourself questions to which there is no answer, such as 'Can I ever be happy again?' 'Do I know for certain that I will get another job?' No one can promise you this. When you find yourself catastrophizing about all the uncertainty that redundancy has created, it can help to ask yourself the ultimate question, '*OK, if this catastrophe actually happened, what would I do?*' Most people can answer this question calmly because some action, however extreme, is usually possible.

Jake was made redundant when the advertising agency for which he had worked for five years went into liquidation. 'My greatest fear was financial uncertainty. We loved our house, had bought it as a bit of a heap and had put years of money and skilled DIY into making it beautiful. I dreaded raising the question with my wife because I thought it would upset her, but of course she had already worked out for herself that we might have to lose it. Sitting down calmly together after supper one evening we had a good discussion where we agreed that we could easily move to somewhere smaller because in the end it wasn't really about the bricks and mortar but about us.'

Autonomy

Although all human beings need to belong to a group, we also have a strong need for autonomy – the freedom to make our own decisions without interference or control from others.

When we work for an organization we give up some of our need for control in order to feel that we belong. Many years of research into mental health at work has shown a causal connection between stress and autonomy. The more autonomy we have, the less stress we experience and the fewer the mental health problems we have. Unless you have actively volunteered for it, redundancy snatches this sense of autonomy away, at least at first. Someone else has decided your fate, has made this important decision without consulting you. Any plans you might have made which have involved continuing employment in that organization have been disrupted. That is why it is so upsetting.

Siobhan had spent 20 years in a public sector organization and was working happily as an Assistant Director. Her aim had been to compete for a Director job in a neighbouring organization. The government announced that all organizations such as hers were to be abolished and replaced by private sector providers. Siobhan thought this policy bizarre but it also overturned all her carefully made plans. 'I knew it was time for me to change jobs anyway, but I wanted promotion where I was. I didn't want to have to change because of some stupid government decision. I was tearful, angry and wanted to shake my fist at someone – but who?'

Relatedness

The clumsy word *relatedness* expresses the supreme value to human beings of being emotionally connected to others. The amount of this we need may vary, but everyone needs some. Work is now one of the most important ways to find friends. I can think of many clients who have told me that they have no genuine friends outside work. The hours spent at work steadily increased throughout the 20th century. Now it is not at all uncommon to spend more than 10 hours a day at work.

You are likely to share interests and concerns with colleagues because you will have been recruited by the same people to work in the same department, so friendships form readily. Redundancy disrupts these relationships. This is well described by Anne-Marie, who was made redundant when the hotel where she had worked for eight years was taken over by a rival chain:

In the hospitality industry you work closely with your colleagues. Leaving meant a tremendous wrench, it was horrible. I knew everyone so well and they knew me. We'd supported each other through all sorts of crises – serious illnesses, babies, marital break-ups, we'd had a fire in the kitchen, deaths, the suicide of a guest – you name it, we'd seen it. I didn't know how I'd manage without that easy, close connection with so many people. I'll keep in touch with some of them but it won't ever be the same.

Fairness

We grow up encouraged to believe that good behaviour will result in a fair reward. We carry this assumption into work, where it is usually described as 'the psychological contract', something different from the legal contract because it is implied rather than stated. *Work hard and your effort will be acknowledged. Behave well to your colleagues and this will be noticed with praise, salary increases and a slightly more important-sounding title.* Redundancy can feel like a clear breach of these unstated rules. You did work hard and gave more than the minimum, you were a loyal team member, you stifled your criticisms of poor management. But now it is as if all this counts for nothing. You may feel bewildered and unsafe, exhausted, powerless and needy. New boss, new owners, government legislation based on political whim, commercial failure – any of these can upend the former assumptions.

I had to compete for 'my' job and saw it go to someone with half my experience and none of my skill who in fact left after only six months because she was hopelessly ill-fitted for it. This gave me a little spiteful satisfaction but I'd left by then anyway.

Management had promised no redundancies if we hit our productivity targets. We did hit those targets but they reneged on their promises. I was bitter that I had believed their lies.

What is difficult about redundancy is that it typically involves all five of the SCARF emotional needs being breached at once, and that is why it hurts so much. You lose your status because you have lost your job, you feel uncertain about your future, your sense of autonomy is removed because someone else has made the decision, you lose work friends and it often feels as if the decision is capricious and unfair.

Gary worked in a care home and watched with dismay as standards fell. Raising his concerns meant that first he was disciplined about the quality of his own work and then was forced to accept redundancy. He says, 'So suddenly I was one of the unemployed with all the humiliation of signing on. I was worried about paying my rent and getting into debt, I missed some of my lovely old residents and the daily routine of helping them – and the whole thing felt monstrously unfair. They'd got away with it – not just how they'd dealt with me but with the poor care they were providing, while the owners just coined it in'.

Surviving emotional shock

The shock people experience can closely resemble the human response to bereavement, and indeed it is a bereavement of sorts because bereavement is always about loss. The Swiss psychiatrist Dr Elisabeth Kübler Ross described the typical flow

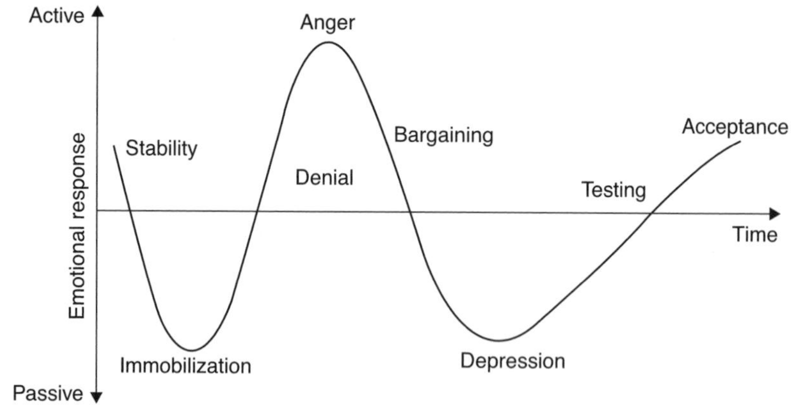

Figure 1.1 Chang Curve or Cycle

of feelings in her book *On Death and Dying*, first published (by Routledge) in 1969, and this has become known as the Change Curve or Cycle (see Figure 1.1). Although her framework has been criticized by later researchers, it seems to me to have an underlying and recognizable truth.

Feelings may follow this predictable pattern, though not necessarily in this order, and they may all happen within a short space of time or be drawn out over many months:

Immobilization: shock, feeling stunned and immobilized. Life feels unreal. You may feel as if you are in a film or watching someone else on television.

Denial: a strange inability to take the news in; carrying on robotically with the normal routine as if nothing has happened; hoping that someone will tell you that it is all a mistake.

Anger: Someone must be to blame for this. It is so unfair, it is outrageous, how dare they do this? The decision is crazy, the people who made it are crazy. You feel weepy, out of control, will talk to anyone who will listen. Sometimes guilt enters the picture here; you have irrational feelings that it must be something you did.

Bargaining: you still feel it's not quite true so there may be some merit in seeing if you can save your job by offering to work for a lower salary or in a different office. Sometimes this may be possible, but if so, this will most probably have been discussed with you at an earlier stage, so the bargaining stage is usually just another way to stave off the inevitable loss.

Depression: a bleak time of greyness and hopelessness. You feel paralysed, unable to shake off weariness. You trudge on but procrastinate about essential tasks such as getting your CV into shape or contacting recruiters, even though you know you should.

Testing/cautious experiment: you begin to feel a little better. You get started on your CV, you see others beginning to recover too, hope seeps back, you begin to get some perspective on what has happened; you believe, though perhaps tentatively, that ultimately you will be all right.

Acceptance: you are now committed to leaving the job and the organization and oddly enough it begins to feel as if this is the right thing to do. Losing your job has given you the chance to reappraise and you have come to think that you might have needed it. You are applying for other jobs with every hope of success or are replanning a different kind of life.

The point about this response to change and loss is that it is normal. When you are made redundant there are two challenges. The first is to avoid the danger of getting stuck at any one stage. This can happen. So I have worked as a coach with people who became attached to their anger and could not shake it off. There can be a perverse enjoyment in rage, in giving way to loss of emotional control, in shouting and threatening. But the more angry you feel, the more irrational your choices are likely to be and the longer it will take to adjust because you are just reinforcing the anger, thus making it more real. Angry people make poor companions; others get bored with hearing the same furious script over and over again.

How to shorten the time to adjustment

The second challenge is to shorten the time it takes to pass through these stages and to get to adjustment as quickly as possible. Sometimes the process can be remarkably swift:

> A client who left her job in exceptionally hurtful and humiliating circumstances, describes a joyful moment of release when she was clear that she was over the worst of the negativity she had been feeling. 'I was walking down Threadneedle Street, a route I'd taken many times before and for the previous three weeks I had felt terrible. But I suddenly noticed that it was a sunny Spring day, the City looked majestic, there were daffodils in the window boxes and I remember the words forming as clearly as if I'd spoken them – *I will soon be free of all this and then I need never go into that awful office again!*'

Make it a deliberate policy to pour out all your feelings by setting aside a generous amount of time and choosing a listener who will just listen empathetically without trying to calm you down or offering phrases such as 'Don't worry, I'm sure you'll get another job'. These well meant clichés actually trivialize your feelings and when people offer them, the usual response is to feel furious because you have not been understood. Someone who listens carefully, nods and accepts the strength of your feelings without trying to rescue you is the true friend (see also page 67).

See this conversation as a one-off, a chance to unload, rather than something you will say to anyone who will listen. The more you repeat your woes, the more entrenched you will become in

the role of victim because you will be reinforcing the neural pathways in your brain which govern your emotional responses.

Focus on the future not the past and especially curb any tendency to replay the conversation where you were given the bad news, for instance feeling humiliated because you felt you did not give the best account of yourself. Invite yourself to get perspective by asking yourself questions such as 'How much will this really matter in two years' time?' 'What are the good things that will most probably come out of a change like this?' 'If I'm the most resourceful possible version of myself, what do I say to myself about this?' Some people get into the habit of ruminating on other aspects of the event, for instance constantly thinking jealously about a colleague who has kept his or her job. If you find yourself ruminating, notice that this has become the pattern and be determined to interrupt it. The simplest way to do this is to change your physical state, so get up and do something different, such as walking briskly for a few minutes.

Avoiding narrowed thinking

Don't give way to wildly illogical leaps in your thinking. For instance, Suzanne was made redundant from her job as a senior librarian and in describing it, she said, 'I've lost my job, I probably brought it on myself somehow, my professional life is at an end, I'm a complete failure'. It took gentle confrontation from her devoted husband to show her that the only thing that was factually true in this statement was that she had lost her job. Everything else was a gross distortion and that far from being 'a complete failure' her years of professional success would stand the test of time and that redundancy did not mean she was a failure as a human being.

There are other typical patterns that can come to dominate the way you think. When we are emotionally aroused, our thinking narrows. First, you should spot these patterns, then challenge them by asking yourself, 'What would I say to myself about this if at my calmest and most resourceful?'

Narrowed thinking	Calm, resourceful thinking
Black-or-white thinking: it's all terrible, I'm a failure, I feel ashamed	Losing a job does not define you as a failure; it happens to millions of people. You have many years of success not just in work but in other parts of your life
I'm a bad person, these things only happen to people who've brought it on themselves	Redundancy happens to 'good' and 'bad' people equally because it is largely caused by factors that individuals cannot control
Clairvoyant: it's my bad luck. It's fate. I'll never get another job	No one can predict the future. Getting another job is far more about how you look for it than about fate
It's not fair	Possibly, but you are over-personalizing something that has affected many others
No one understands	Yes they do. There are people whose professional role is to help you, as well as many others, in your private life
Generalizing: everything is spoilt, our family life, our future plans	Not really: family life can be strengthened and just because plans have to be changed this does not necessarily make them better or worse
Other people will see me as a failure	Unlikely: they see past the loss of the job to the human being. In any case, do you have X-ray vision into their thoughts? How can you be sure you know what they are thinking?

Why language matters

Brain research shows that the language we use – to ourselves and others – has a critical role in shaping our feelings. Don't get into the habit of telling your story as a tragedy in which you are the loser. Instead try using this framework, banning all bitterness, cynicism and negativity from how you tell it:

You are the hero or heroine.

You are a survivor.

There are amusing aspects to the story, even if it is only the comical ineptitude of the manager who gave you the bad news.

There are upsides – this event will allow you to reshape your life and/or career.

There has been learning in it – for instance, that there were warning signs and another time you will certainly be more alert to them.

If you find helplessness and anger persisting, one way to feel better is to keep a journal. Buy yourself a nice notebook and use it to record your feelings, with the aim of tracking improvement. Make it policy to write down the pleasant things that have happened each day as a way of reminding yourself that even at the bleakest times, good things can happen. Overall, the psychological research into shock and trauma shows that the more we believe we can take control, the more quickly we recover. There may be all sorts of ways in which you could do this.

Julie, a manager at a Telecoms company, plunged herself into preparation for changes which had to be made as a result of a merger, even though her own job was one of those going. She says, 'By offering to run workshops for staff on the changes, I felt a lot better. I had credibility with staff because it was happening to me too, but I also had praise from my bosses, and it looked good on my CV'.

Rob, a quality control specialist in a manufacturing company, lost his job when sales plunged because of

competition from China. He posted regular updates on his Facebook page, asked everyone he met for advice and ideas as well as coaching every one of his direct reports in job-search techniques. His comment: 'Just doing this gave me a list of things to do every day and got me over the self-pity phase pretty quickly.'

Feeling in control

Experiencing yourself as in control is vitally important. Psychologists distinguish between people who have what they call an *Internal Locus of Control* and those who have an *External Locus of Control*. What this means in plain language is that when you have an Internal Locus of Control you believe you are in charge of yourself and can affect events to your advantage. You believe you have choices, even in desperately difficult circumstances, because you can choose how you respond. This is the psychologically healthy way to be.

When you have an External Locus of Control you believe you are being driven by people and events that you cannot affect: you are helpless. This is a particular danger for people who have had careers in long-stay organizations, where they have at some level believed that the organization was managing their careers. This was never really true, but the fiction was maintained by opaque promotion processes, as described here by Christopher who had worked for many years in a civil service department before the abrupt shock of being made redundant in his early fifties:

In the olden days, I'm tempted to say the golden days, you were kind of tapped on the shoulder and promoted effortlessly. It was like being on an escalator. I truly believed that someone (don't ask me who as I couldn't have said, but some benevolent force) was looking out for me and knew exactly how good I was

and where I would add most value. Then we had cuts, relentlessly, and the apex of senior jobs got narrower and narrower and instead of the tap on the shoulder we had to be interviewed and go through assessment centres. After five attempts I realized I wasn't going to get any higher so I applied for voluntary redundancy and got it, but my overall feeling was of having been a mug, an absolute fool to have thought anyone was looking out for me.

When your mindset is an External Locus of Control, your energy goes into blaming: the organization, your boss, your colleagues. Most of us faced with a crisis like redundancy will spend at least a little time in the grip of helplessness, but the more quickly you can regain your feeling of being in charge, the quicker your adjustment will be.

Excuses, excuses

Self-sabotage is one of the biggest dangers facing people who have been made redundant. Fear of the unknown quickly provides seemingly watertight reasons why it will be difficult to get another job. The most popular is that recession makes it impossible to find employment, with dismal media stories apparently showing that this is 'true'. While there are many areas with high unemployment rates, especially among young people, as a generalization it is not true that it is impossible to find work. Far more people are in work than unemployed and there are many sectors with skills shortages and companies which have flourished during the recession.

Then there is the age-barrier excuse, and I see many job seekers who make this real by constantly apologizing for their age, looking or sounding years older than they really are or boasting about their technophobia. Employers want skill and experience, and in practice I find that when they see incontrovertible proof that a candidate has these, they care little about the person's age. Other people believe in the myth that they will have to retrain. This is most unlikely: the only time that qualifications really matter (other than in qualifications-led professions such as medicine and the law) is at the absolute beginning of a career when qualifications are one of the few ways to discriminate between young candidates. Yet others are convinced that they 'interview badly', not realizing that virtually anyone can learn how to give a good account of themselves at a job interview. If you believe you will fail then this is an excellent reason for never trying – and for guaranteeing disappointment.

The false goal of 'closure'

'Closure' has become a popular notion. After any major shock, such as a serious illness, a bereavement or a career setback, any number of amateur and professional counsellors will be eager to tell you that it is a good idea to get 'closure' so that you can (another popular phrase) 'move on'. It is true that the more time that has passed after a traumatic event, the more able we are to accept what has happened, to adjust and to manage the pain. It is also true, as discussed earlier in this chapter, that it is essential to let go of hurt and bitterness as constant companions. But 'closure' as an idea conveys the fantasy that there must or should be something we can actively *do* to cancel grief and loss for ever. This is not my experience. It seems better and healthier to understand that 'adjustment' will include eruptions of anger and bewilderment that can still be triggered, even if only briefly, no matter how long ago the actual event was.

Pam lost her job very publically when what had seemed at the time like a trivial misjudgement ended up as a scandal. Her employer created the fiction shortly afterwards that they were reorganizing and that her job was being made

redundant. Pam eventually got another well-paid job, but ten years later can still feel occasionally unsettled and angry. She says, 'When people rake up the story, as they sometimes do, I feel a wave of anxiety and it all comes flooding back – regrets, the fear that I would never work again, anger at the way they treated me by letting the press trample over me . . . It's weird because I really have remade my life and there's no way I would ever want to go back to how things were'.

'Weird' it may be, but it is also human. Better to accept that a major shock does leave its mark rather than attempt the impossible task of 'closure'.

Summary

Redundancy hurts because it undermines our need for status, certainty, autonomy, relatedness and fairness, and there are well-recognized patterns to the human response to change and loss. The task is to shorten the time it takes to get to adjustment. The most effective way to do this is to increase your feelings of being in control of the whole process and to avoid the trap of experiencing yourself as a victim.

Further reading

Dr Robert Leahy's book *Keeping Your Head after Losing Your Job*: How to survive unemployment (Piatkus, 2013) is full of practical and compassionately written help on dealing with the psychological aftermath of losing your job.

To understand more about how the brain governs our emotions, read *A General Theory of Love* written by three psychiatrists: Thomas Lewis, Fari Amini and Richard Lannon (Vintage Books, 2001).

2 EMERGENCY ADVICE

You have just heard that you are going to lose your job. You don't want this to happen. You feel bewildered, overwhelmed. What should you do? In this chapter I look at how to handle the immediate challenges of getting the news.

Organizational clumsiness

Organizations can be perplexingly blind to the misery and indignation it causes to be told something so personally important through impersonal means. Even when the news is delivered face to face it is often done with extraordinary lack of empathy. One of my clients was summoned to an 'away weekend' where he expected that he and his colleagues would be working on strategy for the unit of which he was a part. After what he described as a 'pleasantly drunken' Friday evening dinner at a luxurious hotel, the group assembled on Saturday morning in a large room, one wall of which had two pieces of flip-chart paper Blu-tacked on to it.

> *'This goon [his boss] was actually beaming as he said to us that the paper had the new organization chart on it, with names. If your name was on the chart, that was your new job. If your name did not appear on the chart, you were out and could go home straight away. I remember my blind panic as I searched in vain for my name. I was stunned. The whole thing came out of the blue. I remember gaping at my colleagues. The people who were on the chart looked away. The ones, like me, who weren't, stood like statues. I don't remember how I left the hotel, for instance whether I checked out properly, or how I drove home.'*

In some organizations, where security is a live concern, an employee may have to be escorted off the premises. This is what

happened to Stephen who worked in one of the uniformed services. He had been given various options, including leaving on health grounds or accepting a downgraded job. He chose redundancy and describes the meeting where he conveyed this decision to his boss:

> The senior officer was actually very courteous and pleasant but he told me he was working from a rules-is-rules approach. I was stripped of my pass, was marched by two escorts to the front gate and told that the contents of my desk would be packed for me and sent on. I didn't even have the opportunity to say goodbye to my friends – twenty years of service and it ended like that.

One retail organization sounded the fire alarm to empty the store in order to tell employees that the company was closing and that they had all lost their jobs. Others have received the news by text or email. Even worse has been the many times that employees have heard first about job losses through media reports. I doubt that employers are really as heartless as they so often seem. No one likes giving bad news and it is often easier to hide from the understandable anger, dismay and tears of employees who suddenly find that they will be unemployed. When the media are hot on the track of a story involving a household-name organization, it can be impossible to tell everyone in person because the news is leaking out anyway. When there is time to give the news individually many managers do not do it well: they lack courage, resolve, sensitivity and the skill to listen quietly as well as to talk calmly and clearly about what is going to happen. And even when the whole thing is handled impeccably, the staff member will often feel that it has been a brutal experience, picking on some aspect of it that possibly was unavoidable for the organization, but that felt like an affront.

They were too cowardly to tell me to my face. I'd done 17 years in that company, working closely with the MD as his PA and I was told in a phone call 'to let you know as soon as possible'. I thought it was contemptible.

At the time I could only hear the unwelcome news that my job was going to disappear. At first I was just too upset to respond. When I'd got over that, I blamed him for the way he'd handled the conversation. Much later I realized he'd actually been respectful and sympathetic in that meeting. I was too upset to see it then. I confused the news itself with the person who was giving it to me.

Spare a thought, if you can bring yourself to do it, for the boss who has to tell you. Most decent people will dread having to deliver this news because they understand perfectly well how devastating it can be. Bosses usually feel drained and guilty after these conversations. This may account for the clumsy attempts so many people report of bosses giving the person's hand an unwelcome pat or saying frankly daft things like 'This hurts me as much as it hurts you'(it doesn't and can't).

How to handle the meeting

How should you conduct yourself if you are the person being made redundant? The main aim here as in all stages of dealing with redundancy is to protect yourself: your reputation, your rights, your own well-being – physical and mental.

Ideally you should already have been told about coming redundancies. Employees in the UK now have a right to be informed about business results (the legal details vary according to the size of the company) so early alerting is good practice. You

should have had a written invitation to the meeting and been encouraged to bring someone else with you. This could be a Union representative (you don't need to be a member) or just a steady, sensible colleague or friend. It is a good idea to have a companion as the other person is less likely to be emotionally affected and may be able to hear information which you cannot take in. In briefing this companion, ask him or her to take notes. The role is not to be an advocate for you, just to be there for you and to listen. You will not be in a good state to do this for yourself. Your aim at this meeting is just to hear the main points and to ask for a follow-up meeting later. The manager giving you the news may have an HR professional with them – it is good practice on their part to do so. Ask if this is the person with whom you should negotiate.

Keeping the first meeting brief

Stay calm and keep this first meeting as short as possible. Don't argue, shout or threaten. Issues to establish are: how firm is the decision? When will the notice period start? Who will negotiate the terms? What other help is available? All of these are topics which you will need to revisit in later discussions.

Don't agree to anything verbally or in writing. Say you need time to consider your options. The briefer the meeting is, the less you will be tempted into emotional displays which you could regret later. The more you preserve goodwill, the better you will feel and the more quickly you will recover. Remember that you may want to return to this organization either as a freelancer or as a member of staff in a different role. You want to be able to get the best possible deal, to quote them as referees, to keep the friendships that matter and to leave with dignity. None of this will be easy if the whole process begins in anger. It is much better if you can stay reasonably in control.

As a senior manager in his organization, Max had seen the figures and had already guessed that his job might go. So when his MD called him for a meeting, greeted him with a long face and began with the sorrowful words, 'This isn't going to be easy to do Max but I'm afraid we're going to have to let you go . . .' Max interrupted this speech with the brisk but polite words, 'Yes, OK Tom, we've both done dozens of these conversations, so please don't let's bother with the stuff about my excellent work and all your regrets. Who do I negotiate with?' That set the tone for all the subsequent conversations and Max made an exemplary exit from his organization, on good terms all round.

The manager giving you the news should tell you briefly what the reasons are behind the redundancy, but now is not the time to get into a theoretical discussion about what they are. The decision has been made and it is irrelevant whether you agree with it or not – and it is likely that you won't – but it will not help you to say so.

Ginny was made redundant by her civil engineering company when new owners announced a reorganization. As an HR professional herself, she had actually written an MA dissertation on the human response to organizational change. Despite this, she feels she dealt with this meeting badly. 'I burst into tears. I started arguing with them about how they were doing it, including how they were handling the meeting with me. I challenged the restructure and the reasons for it. I told them they were making a mistake. Altogether I did absolutely everything the wrong way.'

Ask for the employer's offer to be put in writing and sent to you as soon as possible in hard copy to your home address and as an email. If you are pressed to agree a date for a second meeting, say you will be in touch as soon as possible to fix a time that will be convenient for both sides. The employer should encourage you to go home straight away so that you can recover your composure. If they do not offer to do this, just say straightforwardly that this is what you intend.

After the meeting

Review the meeting in a private space with your companion. Ask them to share their notes with you. As soon as possible, write up these notes on your computer. This is called 'making a contemporaneous note' – a more or less instant record of what has been said. Putting it into a computer ensures that it is dated in a way that cannot be disputed. Make a list of the issues that you will want to raise at the second meeting. These might include:

Confirmation that the decision is final: for instance that there are no alternatives – sometimes there are. Occasionally companies can arrange lengthy secondments where the cost of a person's employment is borne by another employer or department, or there may be opportunities for working part time.

Exploration of vacancies: if you want to stay, ask for a list of job vacancies including short-term gaps, for instance for maternity cover. If there are such vacancies, ask to see the job descriptions and if there is anything that looks like a reasonable fit with your experience and skills, enquire into how to apply.

Being 'slotted in': in large organizations like the NHS, restructuring and redundancy is often accompanied by creating an 'At Risk' list where individuals whose jobs are likely to disappear can be what is known as *slotted in* to similar jobs elsewhere without the jobs being externally advertised, though normally there will be an internal selection process. Ask for information about how this will operate.

Exploration of what flexibility there is in the package itself: the employer's offer might just be a starting point, but it may also include an amount of money for retraining, the chance of help with CVs, job-interview techniques, access to a coach – and so on. If these have not already been suggested you should enquire into whether they might be.

Flexibility around your actual departure: you should ask whether they want you to work out your notice or whether you could go immediately, staying on the payroll but not being required to come in. There may also be opportunities to trade holiday days for extra money or to take money in lieu of notice.

Pension arrangements: if the employer runs a pension scheme you should ask what flexibility there is here – for instance for offering extra payments to boost your pension. Part of your monetary package might also be transferred directly into your pension. In effect this gives you a higher payout.

Other benefits: many companies offer benefits such as health insurance, a car and family income protection. It will be worth asking whether you might be able to buy your company car cheaply or if other benefits can be included for a period of time in your severance package, even if you have to trade them for a smaller cash payout.

Share options: these are sometimes part of the total package. Mostly these will lapse when you leave but it will be worth asking if there is discretion here – for instance, if you believe that the value of the shares is likely to rise in the short term.

Legal advice: ask whether the company provides legal advice for people who are being made redundant. If they do not, then it is worth asking if they will cover costs up to a certain amount. The more senior you are the more likely it is that they will agree.

Things to check over the following few days

Check out your redundancy entitlement. This is easy to do in the UK. The conciliation service ACAS has an up-to-date redundancy calculator on its website, www.acas.org.uk. The smaller the firm the more likely it is that they will not have taken legal advice nor have an HR specialist on their staff and might well have got their calculations wrong without deliberately setting out to cheat you.

My company told me that I was only entitled to the statutory amount for the last eight years because they had changed their legal status at that point. But I had actually worked for them for 14 years continuously, for the same people in the same role. Only the company name had changed. Thanks to ACAS I quickly found out that they had to pay me in full and this made a difference of several thousand pounds.

Check your contract of employment. This will state what the notice period is and may also contain clauses restricting future employment. You may want to ask the employer to drop such restrictions.

Check out your tax situation with a professional. There are ways of making any payout tax-efficient, something that will probably have more relevance to higher-rate tax payers, but it is still worth getting advice. For instance, if the redundancy money is paid after you have formally left the payroll you will only be asked to pay a small amount of the tax immediately, giving you the rest of the tax year to help with cash flow. You may also, depending on current tax law, be able to pay some of your redundancy money directly into your pension, reducing the tax liability.

Over the following few weeks

Remember that your main aims are preserving your reputation and making the best possible decisions for yourself. You cannot do either of these if you maintain an angry state.

Is it unfair?

Feeling that your redundancy is unfair and it actually being unfair in the eyes of the law are two separate questions. The most likely grounds for disputing the decision are that the selection process was unfair, for instance that it discriminated against you in some way that the law does not permit, such as age, gender, ethnic origin or religion. Employers will claim that they make the decision about who to keep and who to dismiss on grounds such as attendance record, skills and motivation. More critically, the criteria will be about how far any employee fits the skills profile that the future organization needs. Much of this is inevitably vague and subjective.

Most employers are well aware that the law protects employees against unfair dismissal. They do not want the hassle, bad publicity and costs of fighting a case at an employment tribunal. Nonetheless, employers do break the law and indignant employees do take cases to tribunals. Since the beginning of the recession the number of such cases has risen dramatically.

The case for legal action

The case for going to a tribunal is that it is an independent process, legally binding, providing a neutral forum for judging whether a dismissal is legal or not. Where you feel you have been mistreated, there can be satisfaction in seeing the employer punished. Compared with many other legal processes, an employment tribunal is relatively informal. You have your day in court, and you hope there will be an apology and some extra money to compensate for the loss of your job. You will feel vindicated in the eyes of your colleagues, family and friends, and the employer may be obliged to reinstate you. You may feel that it serves the employer right and that your action will serve as a warning and prevent others from having to suffer in the same way. Sometimes just the threat of taking your case to a tribunal will result in the employer improving their offer. This is because, whether they are acknowledging guilt or not, they would rather do this than risk the cost and trouble that a tribunal involves.

The case against legal action

There are also powerful arguments against. The tribunal system is slow and it can take many months before the case is heard. While this process is happening it is difficult for people to move on: it becomes intensely involving, life narrows to 'the case', absorbing time and energy which might be more profitably spent on searching for a new job. You may talk about your troubles obsessively to anyone who will listen. You may spend many hours assembling documents and may also spend significant sums of money on lawyers, hoping to recoup this with a favourable judgement later, but this is a risk. Publicity, which you hope will embarrass the employer, could just as easily embarrass you.

The financial compensation may be less than you hope, but this will depend on the circumstances and on the legal constraints involved. Where lawyers act on a no-win-no-fee basis, they may also claw back a large proportion of the award and if you lose the case you may have to pay substantial costs. There has been research which suggests that about a third of people who

embark on the tribunal route report depression, with others saying that the process had a negative effect on their physical health. Anecdotally, I have observed that going through an employment tribunal seems to make it a lot harder to get another job. Not only is there the distracting effect of the time and effort it takes, but there is also the impact on employability. Few employers would want to own up to this, but in private many will confess that their dread is that someone who has been once to a tribunal might be a committed troublemaker – in the jargon a 'vexatious complainant'. The publicity that tribunal claims may generate will make it hard to keep the verdict private and, even if you win the case, the suspicion may cling that you were in the wrong.

My own view is that the decision to go to a tribunal is rarely beneficial for either party – but you may not agree.

If the thought of legal action is tempting, there are two courses of action which you might want to consider. First, ask for independent legal advice and, if you can afford it, be prepared to pay for this yourself without entering into a no-win-no-fee arrangement. Some legal advice may be free – for instance, from a Citizens Advice Bureau or a first session from a legal firm. Alternatively, consider a conciliation or mediation service. This is less adversarial than a tribunal. In the UK, ACAS offer a free conciliation service called Pre-Claims Conciliation (PCC).

Working out notice – or go straight away?

There is no one right answer to the question of whether you should negotiate a swift exit or hang on until the last possible point. The time to discuss this is at the second or third meeting when you are negotiating your package. The organization may insist that you see out your notice, or it may be flexible. The more senior your role, the more likely it is that your bosses will want you to leave quickly.

In favour of staying: some people prefer to ease themselves out of their jobs gradually as a way of getting used to the whole idea of leaving. Conscientious people can hate the idea of leaving their projects half finished especially where they are aware that colleagues who remain will have to pick up the loose ends. You may also dislike the abruptness of being at work one day and just being at home the next. You should note that if you are staying, you have a legal right to time off for job search.

Leaving quickly: to my mind the arguments in favour of leaving as soon as possible are stronger. The longer you stay the more tempting it may be to get stuck at the denial stage of the change curve (page 12). Finding a new job takes time, in fact at the moment it takes longer than it ever used to, so the sooner you get on with it the better. On the question of whether you are being unfair to colleagues by leaving quickly, it is usually much simpler to brief them than most people realize. Also, even though you may feel you are being loyal to the organization by sacrificing yourself, sadly it will not thank you for this loyalty and from now on you have to put yourself and your own needs first. Once people know you are going, they quickly stop asking you for decisions or involving you in meetings.

> *I was amazed by how rapidly I seemed to become invisible. People who had been in and out of my office all day long just stopped coming. The email traffic dropped off to nothing much. It was sensible really as almost the whole of my job had been about making decisions for the future and in the future I wasn't going to be there.*

In an organization where dramatic downsizing is happening, an office can become a mournful place, its physical look changing by the day.

The charity had to reduce to one-fifth of what it had been, so it went from 150 people to 30 in just a few weeks. Every day I went in there were fewer desks. As soon as the people left, their desks mysteriously disappeared overnight so in the end there was a big room with a widening desolate-looking space and the people were replaced by archive files dumped on the floor. Horrible.

How to conduct yourself when you know you are leaving

Being made redundant makes you the focus of attention, a lot of it unwelcome. Rather like being bereaved, it is unfortunate that the person who is hurting the most has to do most of the managing of other people's reactions. People will look to you for clues about how to behave. You may feel this is unfair, but understanding the psychological reality will help put you back in control.

'Survivor syndrome'

Colleagues who are staying may well be experiencing 'survivor syndrome', first identified as common among survivors of the Holocaust and observed many times since in the aftermath of disasters. None of this is helped by the ineffectual way downsizing and redundancy is handled in the majority of organizations, where it is rare for managers to be offered training in how to help survivors cope with their feelings.

Feelings among survivors follow predictable patterns. First, people experience relief and even exhilaration – they are keeping their jobs, they feel lucky. Guilt then typically follows – perhaps they feel the leaver has done the job better, or that they should have done more to help those who are leaving. The guilt is irrational because usually there is nothing whatsoever that the survivor could have done and the selection of people for redundancy more often than not has nothing at all to do with performance: everyone knows a high-flyer who was made redundant.

I felt terrible that Nancy was leaving and I was staying. We were doing similar jobs and I'd always been a good friend to her and she to me. I was tormented by feeling that I could have helped her, may be by taking over some of her work, or that maybe I should be offering to go in her place because secretly I felt that she was far more talented than me and the decision seemed to have been made without any reference to talent or skill.

After the guilty phase, it is common for survivors to feel resentful. The focus of resentment may be anything: the people who are leaving are getting a nice pay-off; they will experience freedom while the survivor has to stay in the corporate prison. Most powerfully of all, it is common for those left behind to have to cope with an increased volume of work as the tasks continue to be pressing even though the people who were doing them have left. Research has shown that low morale and reduced productivity typically follow a mass redundancy programme, accompanied by high levels of anxiety ('Will I be next?') and strong feelings of distrust and betrayal. Many survivors will be quietly planning their own exits as a result.

All of this makes it essential to be aware of the traps and to know how to manage yourself through the whole process, up to the point when you actually leave.

Trap 1: Fighting back

The feelings: you are shocked and angry. You probably did not see it coming. This is most likely to be your reaction if you have

been with the organization a long time. Such people often include founders and senior executives who have achieved positions of power through promotion. You believe you are indispensable, and have often been told so by others.

Unwise responses include: calling colleagues to denounce those who have fired you; angry statements to whoever will listen; vowing to have revenge – for instance, by spreading damaging stories about 'what really happened'.

How these responses strike others: unprofessional; you have become an embarrassment, unpredictable; you seem unstable, lacking in 'cool'.

General effect: you will find it much more difficult to find another job. It's a smaller world than you think. News of your behaviour will leak. People will enjoy the gossip but are unlikely to be on your side.

Trap 2: Mourning

The feelings: betrayal. The organization has been like a family to you. You have developed others, protected them from harm, and been at the centre of things as a matriarch or patriarch. The organization has possibly been more important to you than your real family.

Unwise responses include: trying to change the mind of the person who fires you; begging to stay, even on reduced terms; seeking support from subordinates; crying.

How these responses strike others: they are afraid that some of the mud sticking to you will stick to them. Other responses as in Trap 1.

Trap 3: Avoiding

The feelings: you keep them to yourself, or only tell your absolute nearest and dearest. You don't want to cause trouble. It is embarrassing to be in this position. You want to run away and hide.

Unwise responses include: fading away from the scene; leaving without a party; keeping feelings bottled up, losing confidence.

How these responses strike others: puzzlement – but they shrug their shoulders and probably forget you quickly.

Better tactics

Follow the advice earlier in this chapter about negotiating your deal and not rushing to sign anything. When colleagues call, and they will because this news travels fast, do not speak to them or send emails in response to theirs until you have calmed down. No email is truly private so, before firing something off, ask yourself how it would read if it ever appeared in a newspaper or a courtroom, or was 'accidentally' released to everyone in the organization. Screen your calls with voicemail if necessary. Do not speak to the press. If you are in a senior role, as part of the deal, agree a statement with the organization which preserves your dignity. Ideally you should be asked to draft this yourself. However implausible this cover story may sound to you, it is important that you and your partner and friends do stick to it rigorously. Failure to do so is one of the main stumbling blocks to finding another job.

Creating that exit script and why it matters

It is essential to have a simple script which you learn and repeat as often as possible to answer questions about how and why you are leaving. The only people who should have any idea that this is not the whole truth are your closest friends and they should be sworn to total confidentiality, repeating the same script to their own colleagues and friends, if asked. The main reason for doing so is to preserve your reputation at all costs but there are other compelling reasons too, all equally to do with protecting

yourself. The more you talk about feeling like a victim the more like a victim you will feel. The more you talk confidently, the more confident you will feel and in the end you will believe your own story.

After her British company was taken over by a US competitor, with no warning, Marina was told her job would be going and that there was no place for her in the organization. She describes a day of shock and bewilderment, but then abruptly realizing that she needed a convincing cover story. 'My story-script described reaching the conclusion that at 57 it was my last chance to set up a freelance business and that I had decided to leave. None of this was true at the time. However, after I had repeated it 20 or 30 times, it became true and I believed it myself!'

You will be asked questions by people too embarrassed to listen properly to your replies. Some of them may be experiencing any of the aspects of survivor syndrome I have described above and may be unable to manage their irrational hostility. Many people like to gossip and will probe you for indiscretions that they can pass on. Do not fall for this. Three sentences are enough as the basis for your script. The nearer the truth this is the better it will be, but don't be afraid to do a little artful spinning for the sake of your own PR. The essential principles are that as far as possible you convey that there was at least some personal choice in what has happened and that no blame attaches to the organization. This is because the more you emphasize personal choice the more this will protect your reputation as a feisty and resourceful person. The less you blame the organization, the less anything negative sticks to you. This is for a well-researched reason: when we criticize someone else, the listener associates the criticisms with us, not just with the person being criticized. So if you say that your boss was *brutal*, the listener will

remember *brutal* and associate it with you. If you say that the organization was *inefficient*, people will connect you with *inefficiency*. This may be unfair but it is how the human brain works.

So your story should be your personal variants on what follows:

- Yes you are sorry to be leaving and (use whichever line seems most appropriate) it was a shock/you were disappointed at first/it will be a pity to leave an organization you know so well/you will miss so many excellent people.
- You are going to use the time to look around/consider your options/spend some much-needed time with your family/have a holiday/start a degree programme – or go to a new job if you have one, in which case you briefly describe it.
- You wish everyone well and hope to keep in touch.
- If probed just repeat another version of the above.

André wrote himself a 'script' and memorized it with the first letters of each part. 'I had my little memory jog which was SOW. This stood for:

> **S**orry to be leaving, but I've got over the shock now and I realize the organization had to make the decision.
>
> **O**ptions: the one I'm considering is moving to the Hebrides as my wife and I have always been fascinated by life on a croft and we could easily afford to do this if we sell our house in London.
>
> **W**ish everyone well and I'm sure I'll be keeping in touch with everything that's going on.

It worked brilliantly. I used it at my leaving party and in the end it was how I thought about my departure, even though I had been so angry at first.'

Jilly also learnt her 'script' and found that she was able to deal with even the most obviously intrusive questioning from curious colleagues: 'I found that if they asked me follow-up questions such as *Oh go on – what's the real story?* I could just start the whole script up again. They soon gave up. I realized it was working when after a few days people began speaking it back to me, so the grapevine was working my way.'

The party

Always have some sort of leaving party. This matters as it is a symbol to yourself that your time in the organization is over, so it hastens the process of adjustment for you and for others. People will make generous comments to you and this will help you focus on the successes and achievements of your time in the organization. The more senior you are, the more likely it is that the organization will set up and pay for the event. Where you have been in a junior role you may have to arrange and pay for it yourself or hope that others will do it for you. But the rule is: never leave without something to mark the occasion.

Marcus invited five close colleagues to a local pub and told them he would stand the first round but after that he suggested a kitty to share the cost.

Tyler's three team-mates took her to a 'posh tea' in a pleasant hotel.

Stacey insisted on an evening party for 40 people: drinks, hot food, presents, speeches.

Josh paid for the wine but asked the company to cover the cost of canapés at an end of working day party for all 16 people in his department.

> Oliver, a senior manager in a bank, proudly described having had three separate leaving parties: a private dinner where the guests included external contacts from the City, a tea party for his team and a drinks reception for peers. 'I felt no compunction in asking for it' he says, 'they owed it to me after 25 years of blameless service'.

At the party it is important to stick to your script, to keep alcohol to a minimum, to behave graciously and to remember why all this is important. I have seen some people do well up until this point but then give way to resentment and sourness at the party itself. Watching displays of anger is a good source of scuttlebutt for others but does nothing to rebuild your self-esteem. One such person created a 'graffiti wall' where he hoped that people would write sarcastic comments about his bosses, though they were far too sensible to do so. One senior manager had some special tin badges made with the words, 'Stuff You [name of organization]' on them and handed them out to be worn at the party 'as a joke'. This also fell flat as his guests accepted the badges but mostly just discreetly tucked them away in a pocket. Another leaver gave what he hoped was an amusing stand-up comedy turn as his farewell speech but the 'comedy' was bitter jokes about his bosses which embarrassed everyone present and now it is all that people remember about him. It is more than likely that someone will video the event. If you are embarrassing yourself, do you really want it viewable on YouTube for ever?

Summary

Look for a colleague to accompany you to the first meeting and keep this meeting short. Afterwards compile a list of questions to explore at subsequent meetings including the financial package and whether or not to leave straight away. Avoid the traps of

blaming and expressing public anger as these will damage your reputation, and consider carefully whether you want to take any legal action. It is vital to create a simple 'script' that you can repeat endlessly to people who ask why you are going and to emphasize your own control over the process. Always have a party as this helps you accept that you really are going as well as being a celebration of your achievements while there.

Further reading

The ACAS website has a downloadable booklet which provides advice on best practice for employers, but is a helpful read for employees: www.acas.org.uk. ACAS also runs a helpline. For guidance on current UK redundancy law consult the Department of Trade and Industry's website: www.dti.gov.uk.

3 GETTING HELP

Once the immediate decision about redundancy is settled, you need to assemble your helpers. In this chapter I explore who these might be and what you should expect from them.

Friends and family

Friends and family offer the chance to express how you really feel – something that it is usually unwise to do in any other environment. At home you can rant, shout, cry. There is a relief in being able to express yourself unreservedly to someone who is on your side and who will listen. However, it is a good idea to limit how much of this you allow yourself. If it goes on too long it becomes dreary for others to hear. They begin to feel oppressed by your distress because they will feel that there is little that they can do to help.

My husband was made redundant in circumstances that were awful – he was very unfairly and I thought cruelly treated. He can be eccentric and I acknowledge that he can be difficult to handle but he is also brilliant and wonderful. At first I encouraged him to rage and tell me how he felt, but the whole thing dragged on for six months – and then longer again – while the deal was being tied up, I just got frustrated with him. He was repeating the same sentences, telling the same story, still getting angry. I hated seeing him so upset, but I simply didn't know what to do to comfort him and in the end I got tetchy and told him to pull himself together. This created a lot of tension between us with him telling me I was unfeeling and me telling him he was self-pitying and that I was tired of hearing the whole saga described over and over again.

This story has a number of familiar features: the partner at first indulging the emotion, then becoming upset and frustrated by it and, finally, resorting to telling the other person to snap out of

it, forgetting that if it was easy for them to snap out of it, they would already have done so. How do you get around this danger? Assuming the relationships are healthy (and of course they may not be) then people will be sympathetic and possibly indignant on your behalf. But it is not sensible to expect them to give you objective advice because they are not objective.

You can, however, show a partner how to ask you the right questions, without blundering into either giving you advice or getting irritated. Tell them to ask you three questions, to listen without adding any comments of their own and to follow each one with 'tell me more about . . .'.

> What are you most hurt about? (the top-level frustration)
>
> What is it that angers you most? (digging a little deeper)
>
> What are you really worried about? (the core concern)

Once all this has been said, it is likely that you will feel genuinely heard and can then look together at options for the future.

Explain the importance of sticking to your exit script (page 40) and make sure that everyone in your immediate circle understands that they have a part to play in protecting your reputation. When you get to the job-searching phase (Chapter 8) there may be many contacts among your family and wider circle of friends who can be helpful.

Listeners, befrienders, counsellors and therapists

Some charities train lay people in first-level listening skills – for instance Samaritans who specialize in emotional distress and suicide prevention (www.Samaritans.org). These charities are usually careful to distinguish what they offer from professional counselling, sometimes describing what they do as *befriending*. Their emphasis is on non-judgemental listening and acceptance without trying to offer solutions or advice. The service may be

available by phone or face to face. The plus of these services is their ready availability, the patience and skill of the person on the other end of the phone, their willingness to listen without crassly telling you to cheer up or to offer unwanted advice and the fact that they are free. The minus is that the value of what is on offer may vary because the listeners are volunteers and the processes of selecting, training and monitoring them may vary more than the charities would ever like to acknowledge publicly.

The words *counselling* and *therapy* are often used interchangeably but in practice there are some differences. Counsellors may have a shorter training and counselling is generally a service that is offered to people who have been functioning well until some crisis hits them. Like the listening services offered by charities, counselling offers a non-judgemental, non-directive, safe place to explore feelings. A counselling programme would usually be six 50-minute sessions held on a weekly basis. Some large organizations have an Employee Assistance Programme where they offer free access to a counsellor. If you have an Occupational Health Department it is worth enquiring whether this is one of the services they provide.

Therapists generally have a longer and more elaborate training organized and regulated by one of many rival therapeutic bodies. They work with people who are experiencing the kind of long-lasting distress which makes everyday functioning difficult. This will include depression, obsessive compulsive disorder (OCD) and addiction problems, some of which may have originated in childhood. The word *therapy* covers an exceptionally wide range of helping styles, all the way from a full-on psychoanalytical approach where client and therapist could meet several times a week over a period of years, to a short intervention more like counselling. There tends to be more emphasis in most forms of therapy on being directive and finding solutions than there is in counselling. One of the most popular forms of therapy is Cognitive Behavioural Therapy (CBT) where the aim of the therapist is to help the client understand their thinking patterns in order to make some beneficial change in the client's behaviour.

Depression

Any of these services might be useful if you are overwhelmed and stuck in an upsetting pattern of negative emotions, for instance that no one truly understands what you are going through, that there is no hope or that your life is unravelling. It may be difficult here to distinguish between the normal feelings of sadness and disappointment associated with redundancy and the full-on experience of clinical depression: even the common symptoms, as usually quoted, do not seem to me to be of much help since they include things like sleep problems, loss of self-esteem, lack of energy and feeling unable to cope with small everyday tasks, inability to make decisions, persistent low mood or, sometimes, restlessness and agitation. These are all 'symptoms' that most of us can experience at some point as part of normal living. But the more of them appear together and the longer lasting they are, and the more disproportionate they feel to the trigger events, the more likely it is that you need medical and therapeutic help.

Working with a therapist

What happens in therapy? There is no easy answer to this question as it depends on so many variables: for instance, the skills and theoretical orientation of the therapist, the state of mind of the client, the openness of the client to change and on the other forms of social support that are available to him or her. At one level all that happens in therapy is that the therapist asks questions and the client responds. At another, the relationship of trust, the space to think in an atmosphere of non-judgemental warmth creates a crucible where the confidence to change is possible.

It can be difficult to identify which kind of therapist can help most effectively as there are so many rival schools to choose

from. Quality varies enormously. Among my own clients I have heard a wide range of feedback. So a former finance director informed me tartly that, 'All the counsellor did was to repeat my own words. I thought I might just as well have talked to myself in a mirror. It was hopeless, a complete waste of money'. At the other end of the range, a sacked chief executive described his therapist as having delivered 'a life-changing, life-enhancing, totally wonderful experience. After only four sessions my depression had lifted and has never come back'.

General Practitioners (GPs) are the gateway to mental health services and there are high levels of awareness of symptoms and treatments for depression among British GPs. Consult yours as soon as possible if you feel that you have got stuck in a depressive cycle. They may prescribe drugs as an alternative or adjunct to therapy. There are long waiting lists for therapy provided free by the NHS and, as a result, most of the people on a therapist's client list will be paying for themselves.

If you feel that you can afford this help, again, your GP should be able to recommend local practitioners. Look at the therapist's website and see what it tells you about how they describe themselves and their work. If you want to take it to the next stage, it is fine to agree a single session as a way of finding out if you can work fruitfully with this person. The difficulty is that anyone may call themselves a counsellor or therapist – these are not protected names. Ask about qualifications and training: a degree-level course is usually a sign of commitment and depth. Therapists and counsellors should belong to a recognized professional body which has a published code of ethics with complaints and disciplinary systems. You should experience a positive liking for the therapist, feel able to trust them and you should feel safe. If you question whether any of these criteria have satisfactory answers in relation to the therapist you are considering, then it might be better to look elsewhere.

Outplacement

Therapy and counselling originated in the world of medicine and the word *therapy* means *cure* so the assumption is that something is wrong. Therapists and counsellors work with you on your emotional well-being. By contrast, outplacement services assume that you are in an essentially resourceful state so the focus is more likely to be on practical services such as job-search tactics or interview skills.

The word *outplacement* is a clue to how and why it was set up. When organizations began to solve their business problems by sacking staff, senior people were offered professional help to 'place' them 'outside'. The redundant person often did not and could not bring themselves to talk about it and tales abound in the early literature about men, because it was usually men, setting off from home dressed for work, but going instead to the discreet headquarters of the outplacement company. There they would have access to an office with a phone, a set of directories, a list of helpful contacts, the promise to make links for them with potential employers plus an adviser to work with them on their CV and networking skills. In those more luxurious times, the adviser would often be available to them until they found another job.

Today few people need the pretend office and everyone can do their own research and make their own contacts on the Internet. While very senior people may still get the old-style luxury service, today's outplacement companies are more likely to offer mass programmes at every level of the organization, often consisting of workshops to replace or supplement individual help. Some of the individual help may be online or by phone rather than in person. When individual face-to-face help is offered it is likely to be restricted to a set number of sessions, most usually three or four.

As with every other service I describe in this chapter, the quality of outplacement can be mixed. A sceptical article in the *Wall Street Journal* (20 August 2009) described an outplacement

professional chiding a client for ordering cranberry juice, telling her that it could indicate a urinary tract infection and thus give the wrong signals to a potential employer; another described being scolded for ordering a soda drink because it could look 'immature'. Mass-produced programmes sometimes result in mass indifference – the article claims that some research shows that nearly half of those entitled to attend don't bother to do so or never complete the programme as offered. The more the service is focused on senior people, the more likely it is to be excellent where experienced coaches work flexibly one to one with their clients.

It is usually worth attending any workshops that the outplacement company may put on. There may be a limit to the individual help that is possible, but it will be useful to learn from others and to share experience. Some popular exercises on these workshops are valuable sources of feedback. You don't need to be an expert, for instance, to be able to offer a colleague feedback on their handshake. Seeing how others answer typical interview questions can also be a reliable way to learn how to avoid making some of the most common mistakes.

Coaching

Your organization may also pay for coaching as part of your deal, though as with therapy you will be free to make your own contacts and hire your own coach if you wish. The government's Work Programme offers specialist career coaches through Job Centres. Like outplacement, coaching gets mixed reviews. As a profession it is in its infancy. It is unregulated. Some of the people who enter coaching believe, wrongly, that it is an easy skill to acquire and an easy way to earn a living. In practice coaching is notoriously a revolving-door trade with low barriers to entry, attracting people who soon discover that it is much harder than they thought to find clients or to do high-quality work, and who abandon their new profession almost as soon as they start.

There are so many coaches competing for work that it can be hard for potential clients to judge how good any individual coach is. Stories abound of poor-quality coaching delivered by undertrained and amateurish people who are meddling in matters they do not understand.

At its best, coaching can be hugely helpful. You work with a professional coach who has seen it all before, including feelings of anger and betrayal, and who is able to give you 100% of their attention. Unlike your family and friends a career coach can be objective. They are experts in up-to-date careers advice, more important than you might think in a world where so many unhelpful myths circulate about career strategies. My own experience is that reliable knowledge is in short supply about something as apparently simple as how to write the CV that gets you on the shortlist and that even less good guidance is available about how to behave at the job interview. Getting expert help on these two topics alone can vastly elevate your chances of being offered another job.

Getting the best from outplacement and coaching

How can you get the best from outplacement services and career coaching? Here are my suggestions:

Choosing: where you have a choice, for instance if you are paying for this service yourself, word-of-mouth recommendation is best. Where you have this recommendation, probe your contact ruthlessly about *how* their coach was helpful, what specific form the help took and any reservations there might be about the work. Look at the coach's website (and if they don't have one they are not serious about their business) and see how far they describe career-related services rather than just general coaching. Review what they say about training and qualifications and see whether they have individual accreditation from a recognized body such as the International Coach Federation (ICF), the European

Mentoring and Coaching Council (EMCC) or the Association of Professional Executive Coaches and Supervisors (APECS). Are they licensed to administer a wide range of psychometric questionnaires? With what types of client and in what sectors do they say they work? Can they quote success rates? Beware of anything that looks as if it is a cookie-cutter process where every client is subjected to the same rigid system. A warning sign here would be any company or coach who tells you that you must have a certain number of sessions at set intervals of a set length and at a set price. What you need from it will be different from what other clients need and you should expect something tailored for you. It is good practice to have a no-charge telephone conversation first before committing yourself. Approach at least two potential coaches. Listen to any doubts about whether this is the best person for you. A good coach is someone who is not desperate for the work and who can say no if they feel they are not right for you.

Do 50% of the work. Coaching is not a passive process. It is not something which is administered to you like a medicine. If you agree to 'homework', do it. Prepare mentally, ideally emptying your mind of everything else before the sessions. Keep the appointments, arrive on time and expect the same of the coach. Come with your own specific ideas about your goals for the session and expect to be asked what these are. Bring a notebook to jot down any important ideas that occur during the session: this is your responsibility.

Invest enough time. An untrained coach or outplacement counsellor may imply that all the problems of your career can be ironed out in three simple 1-hour sessions. Very occasionally this may be true, for instance if you are already clear about the sort of job you want and already know how to look for it. Experienced career coaches find that this level of clarity is rare. To be helpful you will probably need a minimum of 10 hours on finding answers to searching questions about who you are, what you want and how to find it.

Mutual respect: the best coaches know that this is a relationship of equals. The coach brings their expertise, you bring the agenda. Beware of a coach who appears over-pressing with advice, who does not seem to listen to what you say you want or who makes casually hurtful comments about your appearance, behaviour, skills or previous career. Equally a coach is not doing their job who tells you simperingly that everything you are doing is just fine, or one who fails to make straightforward and respectful challenges. Coaching is a combination of high support and high challenge, but it is easy to overdo or under-do both.

Clarify the contract: how many sessions of what length and at what cost? Is VAT included? Can you contact the coach between sessions for brief catch-ups by phone and email? (It is good practice to make this available.)

Fees: fee levels vary enormously as, like any other service, they are affected by the law of supply and demand. The fee any individual coach commands will depend on how busy, well known and experienced they are, as well as on how many competitors they have. There are regional variations to take into account here too. A high fee does not guarantee excellence but an unusually low fee may suggest inexperience or lack of confidence. Most coaches charge considerably less than their corporate rates when an individual is paying for themselves and you may be able to negotiate a discount if you ask nicely.

Recruitment agencies

Recruitment agencies are only a small part of how people get jobs – you are more likely to find a job through your own efforts (Chapter 8) but it is also worth considering how agencies could help you. The Internet has transformed the recruitment business. The well-known agencies still have high street shops, but all of them also have websites where you can do your own searches. Like every other aspect of finding a new job, it pays to be specific about what you are looking for. A swift search through Google will tell you which markets an agency is targeting. So there are some which deal mainly with PA jobs, others which specialize in social work, catering, construction – and so on. The specialisms may be 'vertical', that is, by sector or profession, 'horizontal' by levels of seniority, or both.

Many job seekers misunderstand how agencies function. Agencies are highly competitive commercial operations. Although it may look from their shop windows as if their main aim is to serve individuals, in fact it is to attract commissions from the organizations who pay them. They are a free service to the individual and make their money from taking a percentage of the salary when they place a candidate. They are in the volume business, concentrating on employers who have many jobs of the same type to fill. They are essentially sales organizations rather than being, as many job seekers imagine, a branch of the caring professions. Many pay their 'consultants' poorly, with a large part of the salary depending on commission. This probably accounts for the bad press they get from disappointed people who assumed that their role was to find the individual a job. This is untrue: they find people for jobs, not jobs for people. The website www.recruiterreviewer.co.uk, where anonymous disillusioned candidates can post their experiences, is a litany of familiar complaints: agency staff who never return calls and emails, who appear lacklustre or actually rude, make promises they can't fulfil, send details of jobs which are a poor match to the job seeker's CV or advertise details of jobs which turn out to be too good to be true.

Where the job you are looking for is a role which exists on a large scale, and is well understood with little apparent variation between the way the job is done, for instance, nurse, teacher, social worker or PA, then one of the well-known agencies may be very helpful. Employers will have ongoing relationships with the agency because it is easier and cheaper to get an agency to advertise and to handle the initial screening of CVs so that the employer can concentrate on the selection part of the recruitment cycle. Where you are looking for temporary work, agencies may be your first call because they save you the slog of hunting the employer yourself.

Zenia lost her job as a social worker with a local authority as a result of service cuts. She says, 'I found a small social work agency in my city, went in to see them and really liked the consultant – who turned out also to be the owner. She spent a generous amount of time with me, made some sensible comments on my CV – in effect de-cluttering it, and suggested that it would be a good career move to do temp work while I tested out my decision to return to the front line. I immediately got two interesting short-term assignments through her, one with a local charity and another with a different local authority. I kept my career going and got some experience which broadened my CV. By keeping the relationship with the agency they got the chance to see that I did good work and through them I got the permanent job I'm in now'.

It would be common to be told by agencies that 'it's very slow out there', or 'the jobs aren't happening'. Don't be put off by this. What it really means is that employers are not coming to that particular agency. This could be because they are suffering in relation to competitors, or that jobs in their sector are declining. It does not necessarily mean that there are no jobs, only that they are not handling the vacancies that do exist.

Getting the best out of recruitment agencies

Choosing. Do your research first by Googling the name of the job you are looking for and the geographical area in which you are prepared to work, and see which agency names pop up most frequently. A specialist agency is probably going to be more useful than a generalist one. Ask around and see who speaks well of

which firm. Your current employer's HR department could also be a reliable guide to a well-run local branch of a national firm.

Safety in numbers. Register with at least four agencies.

Be sceptical. If a job seems to be too good to be true, then it is probably a fiction designed to lure in strong candidates.

Take the initiative. Many job seekers make the mistake of expecting the agency to come to them frequently with juicy job specifications. The best do exactly that, but don't rely on it. Aim to make a personal relationship with one consultant at each agency, be friendly, agree that you will call them or email them frequently and visit in person if there is a physical office nearby.

Be realistic, be careful. Some agencies may have good advice on how to write your CV, and many have helpful websites with free advice on both CVs and interviews. But never, ever, let them rewrite your CV: make it clear that you will do any rewriting and that they must promise not to send it out without your consent. Some agencies are rigorous – for instance, testing typing speeds or language skills – but see these services as useful extras rather than expecting them as basics.

Be honest. Clarify what you are looking for and don't waste the agency consultant's time by waffling and being vague. Don't inflate the salary of your last job – an experienced consultant will see through it straight away.

Head-hunters

Head-hunters are the upmarket part of the recruitment agency world. They differ from high street agencies in a number of ways. They work exclusively on finding one candidate for one senior role, taking a careful briefing about what the employer is looking for. They will not usually be asked to find a candidate for a job paid less than £70,000 and some will not touch a job that is paid in less than six figures. The best head-hunters are able to add value through clarifying what the employer really needs and will challenge vagueness or an unthinking request to find someone exactly like (or as unlike as possible) the last post-holder. They work confidentially through carefully-nourished informal personal networks so once you have a good relationship with a head-hunter you could find yourself acting in any of three roles: referrer, where you suggest someone the consultant might contact about a job; commissioner; candidate.

People typically come to headhunting as a career from successful earlier careers as senior managers or HR professionals. They have been well paid in these earlier careers and can often earn substantial salaries in the head-hunter role, sometimes, like the high street agencies, working on commission and almost always to demanding sales targets. Like their high street counterparts, they only get paid if the post is filled, but they are paid well – usually 33% of the successful candidate's first year salary.

The best head-hunters are thorough, shrewd and hardworking, with enviable contact lists. They can act as a skilled negotiator between candidate and employer, and if you are a candidate they believe to be strong, they can give you pricelessly valuable advice as they will have taken the trouble to get to know the commissioning employer – and the sector – well. So they may give you candid advice on your job prospects, work with you on your CV and on preparing you for the interview. Often they are present at the interview, though without any voting rights, and can give you frank feedback afterwards. It is a much more personal and intense relationship than is usual with agencies that deal with mass recruitments.

Be warned: the headhunting profession can attract outright scams by people who see it as a way to carry out identity theft. If you are called out of the blue by someone you don't know, be careful. A legitimate head-hunter will never ask you for your date of birth, driving licence and passport details or immigration/employment status. If in doubt, check them out.

Getting the best from head-hunters

Head-hunters work on the *don't-call-us-we'll-call-you* principle and it can seem problematical to find your way onto their radar. It is pointless to send them a CV out of the blue: you may get either no response or a polite and meaningless acknowledgement.

Finding the head-hunter. You need to work in exactly the same way that they do: through expert networking. When a head-hunter has called you in the past about a job, even if it was the wrong job and you did not pursue the opportunity, do contact them to update them about your current situation. Ask your colleagues who they know, then when you get the name, call the head-hunter, saying your colleague suggested you contact them – this will make it difficult for them to refuse the call. Ask your HR department for suggestions, again for a specific name, and follow the same protocol. Some head-hunters hedge their bets by placing advertisements in broadsheet newspapers. There will usually be a name and phone number. If it is a job which is roughly in the area of your search, call this person. As with recruitment agencies, don't waste your and their time by contacting someone who works in the wrong sector or at the wrong level. Head-hunters specialize. If your contact turns out to work on a different type of job or sector, ask them who in their company deals with the kind of job you are looking for. When you call this person, again, say that their colleague X recommended that you ring. If you don't like or trust the people you contact, then they are not the right people for you.

Be clear what you are looking for. So if your redundancy means you are focused on a change of career, then say so, otherwise they will assume that you want a job just like your last one. Be realistic and ask them how many jobs of the sort you are looking for they have placed in the past and are likely to be asked to fill in the near future. Don't inflate your salary demands and in fact it is probably better not to disclose salary details in the early stages of the relationship. Listen to their advice about salary and hiring conditions: it is usually well informed, sensible and realistic.

It is a professional relationship. Don't be fooled by any apparent informality. How you answer the head-hunter's questions about what you want from a new job is in effect a rehearsal for future job interviews, so prepare carefully, dress smartly and never, ever, be critical about your previous employer. Aim for judicious honesty on the lines of your exit script (page 40).

Create a relationship with at least three head-hunters in different firms. The chances of any one of them having just the right job for you at any one time are small. The sign of a professional head-hunter would be the one who spots your value and spends at least 2 hours at a first meeting quizzing you thoroughly about your background and career. They will only put you forward for jobs where they see a tight fit between what you offer and what the hiring organization needs. Some will also administer psychometric questionnaires as part of the confidential brief they present to their client at the shortlisting stage. Ideally they will share this with you and it should be a candid appraisal of your strengths and weaknesses as they see them.

Keep the contact going through regular brief emails and phone calls. Often a head-hunter will have early intelligence of changes in the marketplace, for instance of mergers and acquisitions. Keeping in touch means that you are in the forefront of their minds. Stress the importance of confidentiality so that you know you can rely on their discretion.

Head-hunter skill varies. By and large they are not coaches, though increasingly they are acquiring coaching training. However, they should be able to advise you on formatting your CV and on preparing for the interview, though my experience here, based on feedback from clients, suggests that most of their advice is about the hiring organization and manager's background rather than on interview skills in general.

Don't refer to them in their presence as head-hunters. Many prefer to be known as Executive Search Consultants.

Lawyers

Even if you are not pursuing a formal claim against your employer, you might find it useful to get legal advice. This can range all the way from writing a single letter on your behalf to representing you at a Tribunal (page 33). For most people it will only be worth hiring a lawyer if you suspect that by applying a little pressure, you could get a better deal. A lawyer will know how to assess any unfairness and will also have up-to-date information on what kinds of deals other clients have made in similar circumstances. Many of my most senior clients have significantly improved on the offer made to them by their employers by taking this kind of legal advice, including getting the employer to pay for the legal advice.

If you are interested in this route, it can be better to choose a solicitors' practice which specializes in employment law than to go to an all-purpose local firm which spends most of its time on wills and conveyancing, though the local company's fees may be lower. Entering 'solicitor employment law/name of your town or city' into your search engine will usually throw up several names. If you follow the links you should be able to see what the practice says about itself. Word of mouth is, again, a good way of getting a recommendation. Legal advice is expensive and lawyers work on the egg-timer principle, and even a brief phone call might end up on your bill, so you need to weigh any advantage you might gain against the possibility of bearing the cost of fees yourself. A lawyer's instinct is to be adversarial and this is not always helpful. Make sure you see and approve drafts of any letters they propose to send on your behalf.

Your support network

A support network is vital – not just at work but also in other aspects of your life. Write in the table the name of anyone who plays the roles in your life. (The same names may recur.)

SOMEONE WHO WILL	Challenge me	Brainstorm ideas with me	Give me honest feedback	Support me when miserable	Include me in interesting events	Give me new ideas	Listen to my ideas	Remind me of my strengths	Act as mentor and coach	Provide some fun	Keep me in touch with spiritual things	Other
AT HOME/WIDER FAMILY												
FORMER COLLEAGUES												
FRIENDS												
IN THE COMMUNITY												

It is most unlikely that you will have a name in every box. Also, some areas may be more important to you than others. However:

Have you got at least one name in each column?

Where are the blank spaces?

How much do the blanks matter?

Which are the really key areas – whether or not they have a name in them?

What would it do for you if all your key areas had a name in them?

What would you need to do to get more support?

Your core support group

Never, ever, wait for the world to notice how miserable you are, as you could wait forever. You must take the initiative – a rule that applies to every aspect of career management. When you have been made redundant and are looking for another job, you need minimally three people as a core support group. You should consult these people at least once a week. Ideally you need people of different temperaments and skills. Scrutinize the table above and see if you can identify three people whose time you can exploit ruthlessly and who will be glad to be so exploited:

The prodder: kind but tough person who asks if you've done your homework, for instance, carried out your promise to contact three new employers, tells you briskly that you have plenty of talent and should stop feeling too sorry for yourself and will challenge if you feel like running away

The empathizer: listens when you are upset and disappointed and can help you put it all into perspective by reminding you of your strengths

The expert: can offer well-informed help, whether it is legal advice, wisdom about what goes on in particular sectors or knowledge about how to write a CV.

Summary

There are many sources of help when you have been made redundant. Psychological help can be provided by professional or lay counsellors. Therapists may also be useful for people whose distress becomes overwhelming. Recruitment agencies vary from high street firms to head-hunters specializing in well-paid senior roles. Organizations may provide outplacement services or an executive coach, and legal advice may be a way of improving on the organization's offer. It is important to have an informal group of supporters, especially an inner circle of at least three people who can be relied on to give their time freely.

Further reading

The amusing, touching and informative graphic novel by Philippa Perry and Junko Graat gives an insight into what actually happens in therapy: *Couch Fiction: A Graphic Tale of Psychotherapy* (Palgrave Macmillan, 2010).

Introducing Psychotherapy by Nigel Benson and Borin van Loom (Icon Books, 2012) is also a graphic book with thorough, informal and sensible descriptions of different therapies and techniques.

New Coach by Lis Paice (Open University Press, 2013) is written for coaches but is also a vivid description of what is involved in coaching for both client and coach.

4 HOW DID THIS HAPPEN?

Many people who have been made redundant feel angry with their organizations: how come they didn't anticipate their business difficulties? Why didn't they listen to junior people in the organization who had been telling them that customers were unhappy? Why didn't they stand up to the politicians who forced them to make cuts? In this chapter I look at why redundancy happens at all and what lessons there might be for any individual who is going through it.

Underlying all of the current problems is the banking crisis that started in America in 2008. You do not need to understand what sub-prime mortgages are or any other banking jargon to see in the simplest terms what happened. Credit was too easily available, investment banks gambled on being able to continue to buy cheap and lend dear to an ever-increasing number of eager and possibly greedy investors, especially other banks, including the retail banks which lend to individuals. The whole phenomenon was built on recklessly believing that economies would continue to grow and that, for instance, house prices would continue to rise.

But belief is a fragile commodity. The banks lent eagerly to many people who did not have the proper means to repay – and on assets which were overvalued. Governments, banks, businesses, individuals – they all gambled by risking money that they did not have on assets that had become, in the banking jargon, 'toxic', that is, worth far less than the price at which they had been bought. When people stop believing in the myth and ask about the reality it is only a matter of time before the whole shaky edifice collapses, and collapse it did.

These types of crash are not new: they have occurred regularly in the past – for instance the wild speculation on the price of tulip bulbs in the Netherlands in the 17th century, the South Sea Bubble in the 18th century, the Stock Market crash of 1929 which ushered in 13 years of mass unemployment and the dot.com bubble of 2000. The 1929 crash is widely considered to have been the start of the modern phenomenon of boom-and-bust of which our current troubles are just another example.

A wise organization, or indeed a wise individual, might have stood back and seen what was happening, would have refrained from over-expansion funded by heavy borrowing and would have spotted that when the unravelling started, it was not a temporary blip but an unstoppable trend, a systemic problem that had its own momentum. Such wisdom is rare. Mostly, as the history of such crashes shows, human beings want to believe that the good times will continue for ever.

Redundancy is also nothing new. Organizations have always dispensed with staff whenever their own survival has been at stake and the process has been much the same whatever pretty names have been given to disguise what is going on – *layoffs, rightsizing, downsizing, restructuring, reorganizing*. Some grotesque euphemisms have included *Demising* (HSBC), *Synergy-related Headcount Adjustment* (Nokia) *Becoming More Fit* (Yahoo) or *Special Forces Philosophy* (Tesla Cars). What is new currently is the global scale of change and the unprecedented numbers of people affected.

External events as the catalyst

All organization change is triggered by external events. Apart from the banking crisis, the most significant cause is technology. Technology has made it possible for the call about a fault in your broadband to be answered by a young graduate sitting thousands of miles away in a Bangladeshi call centre and working for substantially less money than his British counterpart. A few minutes spent on your computer will show how you might be able to book a holiday at a cheaper price than the local high-street travel agent. Having a brilliant camera on your iPad Mini means you no longer need a separate camera, so the need for a chain of high street camera shops has disappeared. You don't need to buy CDs any more because you can download specific songs from the iTunes store. Sending a paper letter is a rare event when it is so quick and easy to do the same thing by email. Ordering goods online saves the slog of going to an actual shop. Improved technology means that a six-year-old car may still be in good shape so your need for a replacement has declined and if it only has to be serviced every 18 months, the demand for skilled mechanics will also decrease.

All of this is bad news for customer service staff in British call centres, people who work in travel shops, postal workers, sales assistants in camera and record shops, people who work in car factories and supply spare parts, salespeople in car showrooms and car mechanics, among thousands of other similar jobs and trades.

Global competition has been a factor in the decline of western economies for more than 100 years but in the last decade this has accelerated with the rise of the 'tiger economies', and the old staples of the British economy have long been outshone by foreign competitors in industries like steel, cotton or shipbuilding.

The same phenomenon has now affected service jobs. Mass movements of population have been driven by 'economic migrants' – people who are willing to take the risky step of leaving their home country for the better lives they believe are to be found elsewhere. Immigration is a touchy topic in most developed countries where the native population can feel threatened by foreigners who are allegedly willing to do the sorts of jobs and for low wages that the locals will not touch. So in my local branch of the sandwich chain Pret a Manger, there is a rainbow of cheerful servers, not one of whom is British. At the last count they came from Peru, Estonia, Poland, Sri Lanka, Chile and Denmark. The team of carers who work for an elderly neighbour all come from Nigeria or Bulgaria. Whether this is a sinister plot by nameless evil investors to drive wages down or just a natural result of economic forces perhaps does not matter, as the effect is the same.

Political pressure can produce redundancies. Governments fiddle with regulation and structure for ideological as well as fiscal reasons, so for instance a decision to 'reform' the NHS yet again, for whatever reason – 'smaller government', 'efficiency' or 'patient choice' – means there are always going to be losers where jobs are concerned. If competition is deemed to be a good thing because ultimately it is claimed it will benefit users of services, then private companies will take over jobs previously held by public sector managers.

The ripple effect

When the economy shrinks, no one, including politicians, seems to know what to do. Since the public sector is one of the few over which they can have any control, austerity in the shape of severe cuts to services and therefore to jobs, has been the result, rippling out widely. Fewer people in work means there is less money in the economy, we fear it might all get worse and cut back on non-essentials, so more and more businesses find it difficult to keep going. Rising prices and sluggish rises in wages mean that for most of us real income has significantly dropped.

This is especially evident in places which have depended on one major organization to provide jobs. If a large company closes its factory, then many others will suffer too alongside the staff made redundant: all the companies who supplied that plant – from the people who made major components to the young entrepreneur who sold sandwiches from a tricycle outside the gates. In some towns the biggest single employer is the local authority or the hospital. Loss of jobs there will have the same drastic effect on other businesses. Hence the depressing sight of boarded up shops in so many towns and cities.

It is probably true that some of the businesses that have failed might have averted collapse if they had spotted the changes in their markets more quickly. Most of them did try, but the strategic judgements they made proved to be the wrong ones.

Many companies facing these challenges try to do more of what has already failed, believing, incorrectly, that the problem was that they were not trying hard enough with their existing strategies. Failing to spot the flaw in this tactic has defeated many previously thriving businesses.

Individual choices

What can any individual do faced with these scenarios? The more senior you are the more possibilities there might be to influence decisions. The mistake that almost all failing organizations make is to assume that things will get worse before they get better and that essentially the default scenario will prevail, whereas it is actually more likely that things will get better before they get worse. The same is true for individuals. If it looks as if your organization is in trouble, what should you do? Again, it is easy to be wise after the event, but usually there are ample warning signs. Should you bale out quickly or sit it out and hope for the best? Here are some suggestions about how to weigh up the options:

> What signals are there from your organization's environment that the trouble is serious? For instance, is there a growing volume of complaints from customers? Are there hostile stories in the press?
>
> Who are the competitors and how are they doing? Are they taking some of your organization's market share?
>
> What are the business results? If it is a public-sector organization, does it have a deficit and if so how big? In a privately owned company what is happening to the profits – are they growing or shrinking? If they are shrinking, what accounts for the shrinkage? If it is a plc, what is happening to the share price? What views are City analysts taking?
>
> What impact are changes in regulation or the political climate likely to make?

How marketable are your own skills? If you have discreetly applied for other jobs, have you been shortlisted?

When you think about working for competitors, how comfortably does this sit with your personal values?

What would the impact be on your career of either staying put, assuming your current organization can survive, or moving on?

These are not easy decisions to make because you are dealing with high levels of ambiguity and in the end every decision is a gamble.

Oliver was a 43-year-old local authority manager and applied for a job with one of the many companies handling work in his area that had previously been exclusive to the public sector. At the same time he applied for a temporary promotion in his own organization. He was offered both jobs in the same week. After much agonizing he decided to stay put, despite knowing that this was no longer a secure career and that there was a high chance of redundancy at some point in the future. His comment was, 'I am a public servant through and through. When I looked at the other job, the money was slightly less and it was a commercial environment. I couldn't see myself working for shareholders. I felt I was still young enough to make a new career somewhere else if necessary but thought I'd stick it out for the time being'.

How individuals may contribute to being made redundant

This is an uncomfortable topic. The word *redundancy* can cover a wide range of situations. At one end of the spectrum are the mass dismissals that follow the sudden closure of an entire business. There, everyone will lose their jobs including the

managers who have to give the bad news to their staff. It would be common for their HR Directors to say ruefully, 'I am going like everyone else, but I stay to turn the lights out and lock the doors'. In the middle are the voluntary redundancies that are possible when it is clear that the organization has to shrink.

Then we come to individual redundancies, often at senior level and as a result of reorganization. Sometimes these are exactly what they seem: there is no blame attaching to the individual. At other times they are a fig leaf for performance problems. It may be widely known that the poor performer is failing but there is no documentation to show how or why because a succession of managers has been too timid to deal with it or to record it in appraisals. Alternatively, the individual may be performing reasonably well but there is deadly conflict between him or her and another member of the team, or with the boss: harsh words have been spoken and cannot be retracted or forgotten. Occasionally the individual has been a whistleblower and the organization defends itself by either accusing them of poor performance themselves or by making their post redundant. What can often happen is that a sudden change in direction or in the organization's financial results gives a boss the chance to solve a problem that could have been dealt with more fairly and openly many years earlier.

Scott and Bill met as 18 year olds in their first week at university and their friendship developed into a business relationship. Scott was the software expert and Bill the entrepreneur. Starting with one highly specialized product, the company was soon employing over 100 people. They relocated to Hong Kong to exploit markets in China and Singapore and grew to employ 500 people. The problem was that Scott remained unchanged while Bill developed into a sophisticated businessman. There was no bossy wife to tell Scott that his wispy goatee beard, ponytail and

rumpled appearance were not appropriate for someone in a director role, nor to coax him out of his deeply introverted personal style. When Bill put the company up for sale, their Chinese buyers made it clear that there would be no place for Scott. Bill had to choose between the friendship and the business and he chose the business. Scott was made redundant knowing that the redundancy was a fiction and that to all intents and purposes a successor would be recruited to replace him with a slightly different job title but to do essentially the same job.

Scott was, understandably, bitterly resentful and upset about what he saw as a betrayal. No one was ever, even at the point of terminating his employment, honest with him about the actual reasons for his departure. But who was really responsible here? Yes, Bill was at fault for never having had the courage to give Scott frank feedback, but Scott also had some responsibility. People had made hints over the years but he had either not heard or had ignored them. He had refused every opportunity to get some leadership training. He had not noticed how isolated he had become in the executive team, with no kindly friend to take him to one side and alert him to what was likely to happen unless he changed.

Employer choices

When it is clear that redundancies will be made, the employer has the chance to look hard at elements such as sickness absence, performance appraisals and reputation. Skills that were once useful and necessary may now be outmoded and unneeded. Again, it reflects badly on such employers that they have never tackled these issues before, and it can be hard for the employee who is singled out to accept that they have contributed to their own downfall.

Patsy worked as an occupational therapist in her local hospital. Her private life had fallen apart with two marriages each ending in acrimonious divorces. Her only child had opted to live with his father. Patsy fell into depression, had suicidal and vengeful thoughts and began dosing herself every evening with alcohol in order to blot out the pain. Her cigarette consumption went up. She was often hung over and miserable in the mornings, had persistent respiratory infections and took a large number of days off, claiming 'flu', 'a throat infection', 'a tummy bug' and other short-lived illnesses to explain her absences. Interviews with the hospital's occupational health staff had not made any improvement in her attendance record. Feeling unwell made her snappy with patients and some had complained. When the hospital was merged with a neighbouring trust, Patsy was made redundant.

Patsy believed she had been the victim of racial discrimination and threatened to take her case to an employment tribunal. Wisely, she abandoned this course when she saw how much the employer's evidence stacked up against her. Like many others in her situation, Patsy had not seen that her behaviour was widely commented on, that her unpredictable absences caused stress for colleagues who had to cover for her and that people were avoiding working with her.

New bosses often want their own people

The arrival of a new boss can be the signal for staff changes. Some senior managers will make it a condition of signing their contract that they have freedom to fire people in order to bring in trusted associates of their own. Often such dismissals will be disguised as redundancies. The person who is leaving has done absolutely nothing wrong but the new boss sees them as part of the old regime and wants to make a mark of his or her own quickly. People who have been deputies to a departed chief are especially vulnerable here. Although it takes courage and self-belief to do it, and it will depend on your life stage, finances and an estimate of your employability, it is often the best option to offer to leave before you are asked, negotiating your departure as a redundancy, which it most probably is, as the new boss may not want a deputy or will want to reorganize the team around different functions. This is what happened to Caitlin:

I joined a medium-sized publishing company in the late 1980s and, over the course of several years, progressed through the ranks to deputy chief executive. When my boss left the organization and was replaced with a very different kind of character, I could see the writing on the wall.

I met with the new CEO not long after he joined to say that I had every expectation he would want to build his own team and that I would appreciate a straight discussion about my own departure. He confirmed that position and welcomed my candour. Because I had long service and a contract with excellent terms, I knew I would be generously recompensed, but still negotiated hard to ensure that at the margins I got what I deserved including outplacement help. The early approach paid off, and I left with a sense of dignity. I later found that those who didn't seize the moment were treated much less charitably.

Seeing it coming

The brutal truth is that no one owes you a job, years of loyal service don't matter, nor does a friendship with the boss; your colleagues may not fulfil their promises to help you, your employer may or may not behave according to their piously stated values, a business can be wrecked in months by the sudden success of a competitor. Apart from the obvious warning signs of a down-

turn in the order book or the likelihood of a government-prompted reorganization, takeover or merger, signs that you personally are destined for the redundancy list can include:

- Mysteriously being left out of invitations to meetings you normally attend regularly.
- Your boss repeatedly cancelling one-to-ones with you.
- Rumours catching you by surprise.
- Colleagues complaining that there are problems with your team.
- A boss hinting through jokes or asides that you are an expensive resource.
- Getting a mediocre performance review instead of your usual *Excellent*.

The more you experience any of the above, the more you may need to get ready to make your exit.

Avoiding being on the redundancy list

How far do you agree with the statements below? Put a tick in the box that most accurately reflects how you see yourself at work.

	✓	✓	
I'm a problem-solver			I point out where things are going wrong
I'm a team player			I'm a quirky individualist
I look for feedback from my colleagues on how I'm doing			I'm my own harshest critic where feedback is concerned

continued

	✓	✓	
I admire my boss			My boss is difficult to manage
I take the initiative			I follow instructions
I'm cheerful most of the time			I'm often worried and anxious
It's a priority to achieve my targets			I do my best under tricky circumstances
I've opted for substantial training and development in the past year			I've been too busy for training and development in the past year
I will defend my organization to friends			Friends are the one place where I can complain about the organization

All organizations want people who are loyal, hardworking, solve problems rather than creating them, are low rather than high maintenance, are interested in their own development, spread cheer rather than gloom, can work collaboratively with others, are self-aware and add value to the bottom line. They don't like people who whine, do the minimum they can get away with, do 'jobsworth' behaviour or are constantly waiting to be told what to do. If you ticked rather a large number of the items on the right-hand side of the table, whatever the justification – and there could be plenty – then beware: you may be making an impression of being an easy target when that draft redundancy list is being compiled. If redundancy has caught you by surprise this time, then make sure you are better prepared in the future.

Summary

People get made redundant because of business failure caused by recession or failure to anticipate unstoppable trends and to take corrective action quickly. Sometimes individual failures in performance or relationship problems are disguised as redundancies. It pays to be alert to signs that redundancy could happen to you and to be ready to make a move.

Further reading

The BBC's Business Editor, Robert Peston, has written an entertaining and comprehensive book on the current financial crisis: *How Do We Fix this Mess? The Economic Price of Having it All and the Route to Lasting Prosperity* (Hodder and Stoughton, 2012).

Further reading

5 FOLLOW THE MONEY

Money is a pressing worry for most people who get made redundant. The anxiety is understandable. Depending on where you live and on your experience and qualifications, there still is plenty of work. If your skills are in high demand, you may find a new job quickly or it may take longer than is comfortable. Unless you already have an offer in your pocket, you cannot know, so careful budgeting is a prudent tactic.

Wanting more

The truth is that in the developed world, almost all of us already have everything we could possibly need. Yet our brains seem hard-wired to demand more – the latest gadget, more clothing, just one more pair of shoes, another fun Lego set for kids who already have thousands of other brightly-coloured plastic pieces. We have so many possessions that a thriving industry has developed to rent us storage space for all that stuff that deep down we know we no longer need but can't bear to discard.

I grew up in a low-income home, raised by parents who knew at first hand what unemployment was like and who were into recycling and green behaviour before either word was used in its present sense. My mother batch-baked every Sunday, hunted down bargains at the local markets, knitted and sewed most of what she and I wore. We did the painting and decorating ourselves. We grew our own vegetables and literally nothing except bread was ever bought as a pre-cooked product. 'Shop-bought cake' was regarded as a disgraceful confession that you were too lazy or incompetent to make your own. Possessions were carefully repaired; nothing was ever thrown away if it could be reused. The bathroom remained the same for 50 years because as my then 85-year-old Dad said indignantly, 'Why would I replace it? Water comes out of the taps doesn't it?' This stoical make-do-and-mend philosophy seems a little eccentric in today's world, but as survey after survey has shown, having more possessions does not lead to more happiness.

Many of my coaching clients have found that far from being a terrible financial blow, the experience of being made redundant was liberating. Most of what matters cannot be bought with money: time with children and family; walking in a beautiful place; getting spiritual refreshment through attending formal religious services or just meditating at home; doing something for others; learning a new skill. The pleasure of spending is a quick fix and as often as not leads to disillusionment and 'buyer's remorse' later. Redundancy can help put money in its place, allowing you to base your confidence on being a decent human being rather than on showing how many expensive objects you possess.

Nick was made redundant when his magazine decided to put its efforts into online publication instead of print. He says, 'I went from a six-figure salary to nothing. I had the statutory pay-off but, with no proper pension, my wife and I felt we should put it into a pension account and live off her rather meagre salary. It took me nearly 18 months to find a new job so our home-made austerity programme turned out to be very necessary. Having approached it with dread, in fact it was one of the best years of our lives. We turned it into a game: how little could we actually live on? Remarkably little was the answer. We realized how much we had been spending on useless things or expensive entertainment. We slashed our food budget by two-thirds through banning ready-meals, take-aways and avoiding eating out in expensive restaurants, there were no new gadgets for anyone, the children had free or cheap sports in the local parks and sports centres, we went camping in Cornwall instead of to a resort in Barbados. Everyone was fitter, healthier with more energy, slimmer and, most of all, happier because we spent so much more time together'.

Looking at your outgoings squarely

I am no longer surprised by the vague grip so many of my clients have had on their finances, but they would be the first to agree that this is not a healthy way to tackle money worries and in fact I was an offender myself, discovering after my husband died that I was woefully ill-informed about where the money was going. Everything starts with looking squarely, and without squirming or deceiving yourself, at what you currently spend. There are virtually always some unwelcome realizations. For instance, one client discovered that he had been spending a cool £700 a year on cappuccinos. Assemble all your bank and credit card statements for the past year, scrutinize your direct debits and read all the paperwork about regular bills such as Council Tax.

Use this table to calculate current expenditure:

Monthly expenses	£	Essential: can't be reduced ✓	Discretionary: potential for reduction ✓
Household			
Mortgage or rent			
Council tax			
Insurance			
Service charges			
Maintenance: including cleaning			
Utilities: gas, electricity, water			
Total			
Entertainment/media/holidays			
TV: licence and subscriptions			
Internet/broadband			
Phone			
Cinema, clubs, theatre, DVDs			
Holidays			
Eating out			
Total			

contined

Monthly expenses	£	Essential: can't be reduced ✓	Discretionary: potential for reduction ✓
Miscellaneous			
Clothing			
Food and cleaning materials			
Car			
Grooming, e.g. hair, cosmetics			
Loan repayments			
Regular savings, e.g. pension			
Child/elder care			
Medical, dental			
Fitness: gym, sporting clubs			
Travel to work			
Pet expenses			
Gifts/donations			
Totals			

You may also need to factor in expenses that you can see are coming soon, such as university fees, paying for the care of a parent, a major repair on your house.

Now make another calculation. What after-tax income do you have, for instance from a pension, a partner, interest from savings?

Finally calculate the value of any assets: if you own your own home, how much equity do you have in it – what is it worth at current market values, less any outstanding mortgage debt? If you have savings and investments, what is their capital value?

If you live alone then maybe you have only yourself to consider, but if you live with a partner or have children then it gets more complicated. These discussions can become heated, with disappointment, panic and resentment at your joint predicament destroying the chance to have a calm conversation. Where there are strains in a relationship, this is the time that they will show. Following this protocol has worked for many couples, and has enabled them to keep the discussion productive.

1. Set aside enough time: several hours in a quiet place where you can be certain of being uninterrupted. Keep alcohol out of it.
2. Agree a goal for the conversation at the outset, for instance, 'Decide how we can reduce our outgoings over the next six months'.
3. Before you get into the discussion proper, agree what criteria you will use to judge the usefulness of any plan, for instance, 'It should mean we can stay in this house; have at least one holiday; be realistic; fit with what our children need'.
4. Focus on the facts first and keep emotion at bay for the time being. What are the outgoings and income? Clarify any fuzzy areas.
5. Now you can get to the feelings. Each person in turn has 10 minutes totally uninterrupted to say what they most care about and want to preserve in the current situation. The other person summarizes what they have said before speaking themselves.
6. Agree what the common ground is – usually more than either party has realized.
7. Each person in turn, and uninterrupted, offers ideas about possible savings. The other person summarizes before speaking themselves.
8. Summarize the common ground.
9. Discuss how to go forward.
10. If necessary, repeat steps 5–8.

Scrimpers' Charter

Over the years that I have been working with people made redundant, I have collected their tips and experience and pass them on here for your consideration. No one has ever implemented them all and some may strike you as more useful and doable than others, depending on your situation.

Some overall guidelines

The general rule is that no one need ever pay the full price for anything but you have to time your purchases carefully and know how to negotiate. All retailers regularly discount their goods either by taking a straight percentage off or by special offers such as two for one. The crafty shopper does their research in advance and gambles on overstocks being discounted. So if you need to replace a car with a new one, do your buying in the last few days before the new registration period is introduced when the dealer will be desperate to unload remaining stock. Buy children's school clothing and stationery in early August when there are often two for one deals. For household linen it is hard to beat the big retailers' special buys when they order bulk purchases of high-quality plain sheets, duvets and towels to be sold in January and July sales.

In general, if the seller wants to shift their stock or make the sale more than you want that particular product, then you will have the advantage, and vice versa. To negotiate you have to lose any embarrassment about haggling or fear of being rejected. Always research the market first so that you know exactly what you need and the range of prices that comparable goods and services can command. Never tell the salesperson what your budget is, even if they ask, as they will then offer you full price goods to match your budget rather than the higher specification product you may have your eye on. Be realistic – your market research will come in handy here – and be prepared to walk away if the price does not match your needs. Dialogue that works will include:

> *Yes, I do like this [whatever] and I can see that it's got a lot of what I need, but I expected to pay less.*

I see that something very similar is on sale at [wherever] for [less]

I do like it but [you name some flaw: it's a funny colour, has a mark, is last season's stock . . .].

What room is there for some compromise on price?

What's the best you can do on price?

How about splitting the difference?

If I were to buy this, what else might you throw in?

These tactics will work whether you are haggling over a book with a stall holder at a car boot sale or buying a house.

Credit and finance

You may have to use up your redundancy pay-off just to keep going. If you are fortunate enough to be able to set it aside, it is wise to get professional advice. It makes no sense to leave a large sum in your current account where inflation will erode its value. If you possibly can, avoid credit, and especially avoid so-called payday loans, which can turn a debt of £100 into a terrifying sum running into thousands of pounds a year later.

The new science of 'behavioural economics' shows what we all already know, that the more space and time there is between buying and paying, the more recklessly we will spend. If you had to pay for everything you bought with hard cash, what would you actually buy? Substantially less of everything is the probable answer. By postponing the moment of payment, some research suggests that we will pay up to twice as much for the same product than if we were paying with cash on the spot. Some retailers and service providers will also add 1–2% on to your bill if you pay with a credit card, and using a credit card for cash withdrawals can cost up to 5% extra.

Rani was made redundant from a job which had only ever paid a modest salary. After a sobering discussion about budgeting and spending, she found that doing without a credit card was one of the secrets to survival on a much smaller income: 'My husband and I agreed that we would cut up our credit cards so that there was no temptation. This had an amazing impact on our buying habits. We kept one debit card to make occasional online purchases and to withdraw cash and used that for everything. Result: we were able to track our spending. Even though I got a new job quickly we've never gone back to credit cards.'

If you already have credit card debt, it might be better, depending on your circumstances, to arrange a discussion with your bank about consolidating it into a loan which you can pay back on a regular basis. What does not work is a hope-for-the-best approach where the underlying worry is far worse than facing the truth and planning to deal with it.

Stuff

Go to any car-boot sale, look on eBay, and you will see the tragic evidence of our obsession with Stuff that we don't need. I guarantee that you will find sandwich toasters, tea-makers, electric knives, foot spas, coffee machines and kitchen scales, some of them still in their boxes, promises of a sophisticated life where you soak your feet in perfumed bliss, make delicious toasted sandwiches from exotic recipes and loll in bed while a machine makes your early morning tea. None of this ever really happens. The Stuff does not earn the space it takes up and eventually gets junked.

When you get made redundant and have to assume tight control over your budget, you get the opportunity to break free from the craving to buy. If you are tempted to give way, you might want to experiment with the tactic developed by one client who uses the acronym **WAIT**. This stands for **W**alk away for half an hour to give yourself space rather than giving way to impulse buying. **A**sk: why am I attracted to it? Is this really just a response to clever marketing? **I**nquire into what problem I believe possessing it will solve for me. **T**hink: do I really need this rather than just wanting it?

Other useful questions to postpone or manage the impulse to buy are

> *Do I already have something just like this which could be updated or repaired?*
>
> *What will I give away to make storage space for this object?*
>
> *Could I hire, borrow or exchange something just like it rather than actually buying it?*

When you really do need Stuff, then consider turning other people's mistakes to your advantage. Local auction houses and eBay sell good quality furniture for a fraction of what the same thing would cost new. Car-boot sales are another good source, particularly of kitchen equipment, cutlery and crockery – but go with a shopping list to prevent impulse buys – and be wary of electrical goods unless you can be certain that they are safe.

Many perfectly usable objects are discarded because they have some small fault that can be remedied with simple repairs, refurbishments and replacements. One client with high-level DIY skills and little money equipped his flat almost entirely from free or very cheap discarded furnishings, refashioned by him into something smart and comfortable. He did this by monitoring Freecycle constantly, by roaming the streets looking for things people had thrown out on to pavements or into skips, and also found a dump where an enterprising council sorted out reusable objects and sold them at the gates for knock-down prices.

Clothing

In the past, clothing was cherished because it was special. Sometimes it was so special that it could be left to others in your will. Fashions changed slowly. Now we have Primark, Topshop, H&M and other retailers who sell ultra-cheap clothing where new lines are added every week. So if you wish, you can save a lot of money on your clothes budget by doing all your shopping in budget stores. This can become a dismal experience as – how to say this politely – the quality is not wonderful.

Instead of buying a major new item of clothing, it is often simpler and cheaper to declutter ruthlessly and then to update what you already have with different accessories or combinations. Rather than buying yet more ultra-cheap clothes, you might want to search charity shops for high-quality items that can become staples in your wardrobe. Charity shops now compete with dress agencies (euphemistic word for sellers of second-hand clothing) for quality and price. The best charity shops are professionally set out, their stock carefully selected and shrewdly priced. A charity shop in an affluent area will generally have better stock than one in the poorest neighbourhoods.

Part of my work as a coach is to offer people colour and style advice. This is not about fashion: it is about ensuring that the image people want to project is consistent with how they actually look. I find that my clients are no different from the majority of the population in wearing 20% of their wardrobes 80% of the time – in other words, their cupboards are crammed with hoarded clothing that they never wear. Ideally you want to change this so that you wear 80% of your wardrobe 80% of the time.

Making money from your discards

You can raise money through selling unwanted goods on Internet auction sites. The people who do this most successfully are those

who see it as a fun way to run a small shop with no overheads. It would not be fun to me to take photos, buy wrapping materials, trudge to the post office and deal with returns, but I know people who relish it. Perhaps they are the same people who like selling at car-boot sales and don't mind standing about on a cold day while haggling with buyers over what are already small sums of money. The benefit is more likely to be the satisfaction of clearing away clutter than making any huge financial gain.

Food and household consumables

Increases in food prices are one of the most obvious ways in which inflation has eroded disposable income. You have to eat, but the truth is that you may eat better when you are forced by redundancy to reconsider your food budget. Eating habits have changed enormously in the past 30 years. It is becoming rarer to eat together around a table. As cookery shows on TV have multiplied, confidence in our cookery skills has declined. Maybe we are intimidated by all that cheffy expertise or else it is just too easy to buy something ready-made.

It is remarkably simple to cut your food budget and at the same time to eat better than ever. Many ready-meals still contain high levels of salt, sugar, saturated and transfats, all of these bad for our health. Cooking from scratch will save you anything from half to three-quarters of the cost of the same thing as a ready-meal. A luxury soup presented in an attractive container, perhaps with olde-worlde cottages on the label and called something like Aunty Flo's Home Made Yummy Onion Soup, can be made at home for pence and will take only minutes to prepare. And you will know exactly how much salt and fat has gone into it.

Antony's experience shows that even a nervous beginner cook can do this. As a single man living alone, he was used to a lot of rather grand eating out or just going to Marks &

Spencer to buy something to microwave when at home. He says, 'At 56 I realized it could take me a while to get another job and that my pay-off would not last for ever so I had to economize. I knew literally zilch about cooking. I bought a short paperback cookery book aimed at students as I thought the author would know about guys like me. I didn't have any decent knives and I'd never chopped an onion. But I started with spag bol and went on from there. I found I enjoyed it a lot and it shocked me how very much more cheaply I could make delicious food than buying it in a supermarket. I cooked a fantastic Sunday lunch from scratch including home made bread for eight friends last week and I've progressed from my student cook-book to Heston Blumenthal!'

Many of us stockpile tinned and dried food that we will never use. If you don't actually eat baked beans there is no point in buying several tins on special offer 'just in case'. In preparing to write this chapter I did an archaeological survey on my own cupboards and among other shaming discoveries there was a 10-year-old packet of dried cannelloni tubes, clear evidence that I will never be the type of person, keen cook though I am, to fiddle around with stuffing any kind of pasta. We throw away a shockingly large amount of food – some surveys have calculated that this might be as much as a third of what we buy. Again, if you now have more free time, you can prevent yourself paying for food you never use by shopping more frequently and more carefully.

Street market fruit and vegetables can be anything up to 60% cheaper than the same thing fancily packaged in supermarkets. Shopping for seasonally available produce allows you to take advantage of gluts in crops when prices are low. If you do buy your fruit and veg in a supermarket it is cheaper to buy it loose than packaged. When supermarkets have special offers, think

carefully before buying: will you really use that third pack of mince? The answer could be yes if you do some bulk cooking and freeze what you don't immediately need.

Whether you shop in a supermarket or a street market, make a list and stick to it. Wandering around hoping to be prompted by those attractively stacked shelves is exactly the way that retailers persuade us to spend more than we intended. If you are doing a top-up shop, take a basket not a trolley. This works on the same principle that one of the best ways of losing weight is to use a smaller plate: it looks full so you don't add more than you really need.

Bulk buying can save a lot of money as long as what you buy is not perishable and you have somewhere to store it or have a friend who will split the delivery with you. Buying a vast sack of my cat's favourite dried food online when the retailer has a promotion offering 10% off and free delivery saves me around 35% of the cost of buying the same thing in smaller quantities. A colleague has joined Costco and buys cleaning, laundry and hygiene products from them in bulk and at a considerable discount.

Travel

With rail travel there is no doubt that it is cheaper to book online and in advance on a named train. If you also choose a train that is outside business travel hours it is cheaper still, sometimes as little as 10% of the standard price. Even if you book only a day in advance this can be cheaper than turning up on the day and buying at the station. Sometimes split ticketing (buying separate tickets for each leg of the journey) can save substantial amounts. Rail cards soon recoup their cost for family or senior travel, usually netting a 33% discount, making train travel far more affordable especially if, again, you travel outside peak hours. Bus travel is cheaper still and long-distance travel bus companies have learned to copy the feel, tone and customer care of airline travel. Over shortish distances they may be just as comfortable and take little longer at half the cost of the train.

Fun and leisure

Depending on where you live, much fun can be had for free. Our magnificent museums have no entrance fees; most cities have free or cheap gigs, festivals and concerts especially in the summer. Logging on to websites like SeeFilmFirst can produce last minute invitations to free film previews and many cinemas have two-for-one offers on set nights of the week.

In a previous home, we had crammed bookshelves everywhere. In the end I felt oppressed by those thousands of books, hardly any of which I was ever likely to read again, and when we moved it was a relief to ship most of them to Oxfam. Although books feel special, in fact they are just another type of Stuff and it is easier to borrow than to buy either in a bookshop or electronically. We have to hope that public libraries will survive cuts – my local branch is magnificent with ultra-efficient free online ordering and friendly service.

Eating out is expensive but you can reduce the cost by logging on to websites like Voucher Codes and getting alerts to special offers. These can reduce the cost substantially. Similarly if you are prepared to eat early, many restaurants have 'theatre menus' where in return for a more restricted choice you get a bargain price.

It is important to keep up an exercise regime when you have been made redundant as there is no doubt that exercise is a mood-improver. However, gym membership can seem like a luxury when you are watching your budget, and there is plenty of evidence that gyms make their money from people who start off with the best intentions and then rarely go. Many of my clients have found perfectly good alternatives:

When I did the sums I realized I'd been paying Fitness First £40 per swim – madness. Walking briskly was free and just as good for me.

A friend is a personal trainer and he set me up with a series of routines I could do at home – e.g. with a resistance band, some hand weights, etc. The principles were exactly the same.

Gifts

Many people who have lost their jobs through redundancy feel shamed and embarrassed that they can no longer buy lavish gifts.

My niece was getting married and I felt awful that I just couldn't buy her an expensive present. Looking at the John Lewis list brought it home that others were spending hundreds – it was all so public.

Christmas was horrible. Previously I'd gone a little crazy and indulged everyone, especially the children. Now I couldn't.

However, let's take a different view here. Present-buying can be just another example of our tendency to buy things no one really needs in order to convey an attractive image of ourselves, or even to control other people by buying something that we think will improve them, the most grisly example of which is surely a husband who gives his wife a gift voucher for plastic surgery. Research has shown that if recipients are asked to guess how much a present has cost they will consistently undervalue it by about 50%. Department stores like John Lewis have whole areas devoted to pointless presents where the packaging probably costs almost as much as what is inside.

Why give presents? One reason is to give a symbolic representation of your affection for the recipient. This can be done as easily with little or no money as with a budget of hundreds. For instance, making it yourself can produce personalized gifts like food presents and toys at low cost. A client with little money learnt how to do bookbinding and produces exquisite hand-made books as presents for friends, using collage and his own drawings. You might also consider giving away some pleasing object you already possess to a suitable recipient: for instance, a lovely piece of jewellery or a beautiful bowl.

Research into happiness suggests that a planned pleasant experience is more enjoyable than acquiring a physical object. The pleasure is more intense and lasts longer. Ideas for gifts that exploit this phenomenon could include setting up a whole day of low-cost treats for children; gifting a day of joint gardening where home-grown plants are re-potted; organizing a 'mystery tour' to take in a number of beauty spots.

While I was looking for a new job and had to watch every penny, I just told everyone straight that I couldn't spend lots on presents. Instead, I did fabulous free or cheap days out – so for the 7-year-old's birthday we took the boat to Greenwich, played in the park, admired the Cutty Sark *from the outside, had a picnic. Great day out and cost roughly a fifth of what I was formerly spending on his present.*

My dear old Dad really didn't need another useless scarf or a new electric blanket as a birthday present. Instead we drove to one of his favourite places on the cliffs, had a nice natter, then a pub sandwich and went home: perfect.

'It's the thought that counts' is so true. It really is not about money. It is about time, thought for the recipient – and love.

Summary

Being made redundant does create fear about money, but it also gives you the chance to assess your financial status generally

and to review what your real needs are. Economizing need not mean deprivation and often leads to unexpected bonuses such as living more healthily and getting free of the compulsion to buy stuff that you do not need and will rarely use.

Further reading

Enough. Breaking Free of the World of More by John Naish (Hodder and Stoughton, 2008). A book which challenges our need for more, including more information, more ambition, more food, more happiness.

Predictably Irrational by Dan Ariely (HarperCollins, 2008). A readable introduction to behavioural economics, reporting experiments into our buying habits.

6 WHAT YOU WANT, WHAT YOU OFFER

I cannot think of many clients who have gone through redundancy and who have had many moments of regret about it later. 'Later' may mean several years or only a few weeks. This has been true even when, at the time, the parting felt agonizing or when the lost job felt like the ideal job.

I always felt lucky to work for the BBC – what a fabulous organization, so many clever people. I loved my work and to be made redundant was a terrible blow, but actually now I wonder why I stayed so long.

When I had lunch with a former colleague a few weeks ago and she was telling me about the horrible atmosphere of fear and recrimination because more redundancies were expected at any moment, her eyes widened as I told her that in my new company our problem was finding enough people to make our rapid expansion plans possible. I was very loyal to my old organization, I hadn't wanted to go, but I now I am so very glad to have left.

The main reason that people report feeling so upbeat about having left is that the forced departure has compelled them to rethink their lives and careers. This may be especially true when they have stayed a little too long in one place. Usually this has happened because the work is enjoyable and the people congenial, so if it is a rut, it is a pleasant one. The longer you stay in the same organization, the more you may also feel institutionalized, with secret doubts about whether you would find a job elsewhere, so fear of rejection keeps you stuck. Being tipped out into the marketplace is a way of confronting unmet needs and rethinking all aspects of your life.

Why 'Who will have me?' is the wrong question

In their initial panic at losing their jobs, the first question many people ask themselves is, *Who will have me?* This is the wrong question and can easily lead to rushing into a new job just because it is something, anything, and it will pay the bills. Instead of leading to satisfaction it can turn into a repeat of all the dreary aspects of exactly what you hated in the previous job. Sometimes, this might be the right thing to do, but only after giving careful thought to a much more important question: *What do you really want?*

Losing a job can give the chance to reassess priorities. *Have I been too much in love with work at the expense of my friends and family? Have I been neglecting my health because I've been telling myself I don't have time? Have I been doing a dreary job because I'm too scared to go for something more challenging?* Often what happens is that we are just carried along by our current preoccupations and work on the principle that we will get around to rethinking it all one day. Redundancy may give the chance to start again or at the very least to make more conscious choices.

How happy are you with your non-work life?

Research into happiness consistently shows that above a certain modest level, more money does not make people happier, and also that lasting happiness is more about giving than getting. Rather than starting with work, you might want to consider what else is going on in your life. This may reveal areas that you need to consider when thinking about your future. Fill in this quiz as a way of finding the answer to the question: *Where does work need to fit with the rest of my life?* rather than *Where does the rest of my life need to fit with work?*

Put a tick in whichever column represents an honest appraisal of the non-work parts of your life. Where you have ticked column 3, use the Comments column to jot down what would

need to change to get more of what you want. Then highlight any areas that have priority importance for you.

	1. Happy with what I have	2. OK	3. Would like more; could be better	Comments
Leisure activities				
Fun				
Fitness				
Health				
Partner				
Parents				
Other family				
Friends				
My home				
Learning and development				
Spiritual growth				
Community involvement				

Here is how one person responded after filling in this questionnaire:

Fliss had had a long management career in a utilities company. Redundancy gave her the chance to reconsider her whole life. 'I'd been a working mum and felt that typical guilt. My children were teenagers and needed more attention. My parents were in their late eighties. I had neglected fitness, giving myself the excuse of my long days and senior role. "Community involvement" gave me a guilty start as there was none in my life. My solution has been to opt for part-time interim work. I'm busier than ever as I'm now a school governor, do voluntary work as a mentor to young offenders and spend a day a week with my Mum and Dad. I have less money, though funnily enough not a lot less, but a huge amount more satisfaction in my life.'

I do not want to imply any 'shoulds' or 'musts' about your conclusions in assessing your life. A significant minority of my own clients is utterly clear that they love their work, work entirely shapes their identity, gives them enormous satisfaction and everything else is secondary. As one said, 'I need to earn enough to pay others to do the domestic stuff that I'm no good at and can't stand'. This is a choice; they make it with 100% awareness of the consequences and it is the right choice for them.

Short cuts to understanding yourself

A good psychometric questionnaire can give you a reliable short cut to understanding yourself, helping you rule out jobs that would obviously be a poor fit and rule in possibilities that would match your temperament and needs. Ideally psychometric questionnaires are best administered by a trained and licensed coach, but reasonable alternatives are available free on the Internet. Please note, though, that no questionnaire can tell you everything about yourself nor is there any magic solution where you complete a series of questionnaires, click on *submit* and out comes a report with the name of the ideal job for you on it. The purpose is to get more clarity, not to find some kind of final answer to the mystery of what your next job should be.

Psychologists have agreed that there seem to be five main factors in human personality, labelling them Openness, Conscientiousness, Extraversion, Agreeableness and Neuroticism. A good all-round version of a 'Big Five' personality factor questionnaire is the one developed by Dr Lewis Goldberg and Professor John Johnson. Taking it gives you an instant free report. http://www.personalitytest.net/ipip/ipipneo300.htm

The Myers Briggs Type Indicator (MBTI)® is a well-known personality questionnaire which sorts people into 16 types. Only licensed practitioners can buy the MBTI but there are free alternatives, one of the best of which is the Keirsey Temperament Sorter. http://www.keirsey.com/sorter/register.aspx

In the past two decades there has been increasing interest in identifying and working from strengths rather than focusing on weaknesses. One of the best questionnaires here is the Values in Action survey. Again, you get an immediate report. https://www.viacharacter.org/surveys.aspx

Interests and enthusiasms

For most of us there are certain interests and concerns that simply won't and don't go away. Knowing what enthuses you points to what motivates you and often that will in turn point to skills that are valuable to an employer. This will include apparently humble skills and interests which you may undervalue. Ask yourself these questions:

What did you always find easy as a child – things that other children struggled with?

Which school subjects absorbed you?

Which achievements in your life give you most pride?

Thinking about courses you have done, which ones stick in your mind as having had a major impact on you? What was it about them that had that effect?

If you could invite anyone, living or dead, real or fictional, to a supper party, who would be there? What is it about each one that you admire?

You have a year fully funded with no money worries; how would you fill your time?

Assume for the moment that every job pays at the same rate; what would you choose to do?

Thinking about your skills, is there one or more that you would do or pursue, regardless of whether you get paid for it?

Which sections of a newspaper/iPad or phone app do you turn to first and read most carefully?

You are a TV scheduler for an evening and can pick any mix of programmes that you fancy. What programmes do you choose?

You can select any expert on any subject anywhere in the world, free, to deliver one-to-one training/learning for as long as you like. Who would it be? What would you learn? Why would this learning matter so much to you?

Answering these questions is liberating; it often suggests interests and concerns which indicate knowledge, skills and talents which simply must be used.

Career trends

Although it can feel as if a career has been random, with strange leaps between sector or types of job with choices made through lucky encounters, in practice I find that this is only superficially true. When you look more carefully, most people's careers have a clearly discernible thread. So an early poor choice of job will have told you clearly what you don't like and the haste with which you scrambled out of it to something more congenial will be a strong clue to what your real career needs are.

This exercise asks you to track your career choices by looking at what led you into each job, what you enjoyed most in it and what was behind your decision to leave. What you hoped for when you joined, high spots of actually doing the job and any boredom or disillusionment on leaving will be markers indicating what really motivates you. Take a large piece of paper and divide it into four columns. Factors to consider might include the reputation of the organization, money, status, opportunities to learn, relationships with others, the physical environment in

which you would be working, security or excitement, opportunities to use favourite skills – and so on.

Name of job/dates	Reasons you joined	What you liked most in the job	Reasons you left

Finding your career anchor

The writer and career specialist Professor Edgar Schein suggests that in any career and life, there is one overriding motivator or driver. This driver is supported by core skills and underpinned by deeply held values. These link to our life purpose, whether or not we are conscious of it. Discovering your most important motivator is therefore critical. It can help you identify what direction you should take after a forced career move and decide which path to take when you have what look like equally attractive options open to you.

Schein calls these core motivators *career anchors*. They help distinguish between what he calls the 'external career' – the actual jobs and qualifications that form the externally visible stages in a career – and the 'internal career'. The internal career is driven by the real values, talents and motivators that we all have. Schein suggests that there is always one core driver that represents the foundation of who we are: the one thing we would never willingly give up.

The eight anchors

Read the descriptions that follow. There is no better-than or worse-than anchor. All have value. At the end of each, give points out of ten for how far this anchor describes you.

1 *Technical/Functional Competence.* You enjoy being expert in your own area and exercising that talent. You need to continue to get better and better at it along with a high level of autonomy within agreed professional goals. Where reward is concerned you prize further training and development, sabbaticals and study leave. Promotion: ideally you would prefer to head up your functional specialism rather than to become a general manager. You resent being asked to give up specialism but might be willing to hang in there with an organization if it allows you to go on being expert in your field and to pay you more while doing so.

Points out of ten for how far Technical/Functional Competence describes you:

2 *General Managerial Competence.* You enjoy running a significant part of the organization and you like accountability. You relish taking responsibility for big decisions. Often you will have left a specialist job in early career to move into a managerial role. You need chances to identify and solve the organization's problems, to cut through the detail to get to what really matters. You are stimulated by organizational politics and are irritated by people who block change and lack corporacy. You expect reward to be fairly based on measureable results. You also expect promotion frequently and look forward to it because you will get more responsibility. Being promoted is in itself a reward you value along with status symbols such as money, a decent office or a car.

Points out of ten for how far General Managerial Competence describes you:

3 *Autonomy/Independence.* You are one of life's natural free-lancers. You enjoy freedom from other people's rules and regulations. You need project or contract work that allows you the freedom to come and go on time-limited assignments. You have self-reliance and are not easily swayed by others. You are irritated by bureaucracy, petty rules or close supervision and dislike offers of golden handcuffs. You judge reward by how far it is portable and has no strings attached. Promotion doesn't interest you much, especially if it involves a loss of your treasured freedom.

Points out of ten for how far Autonomy/Independence describes you:

4 *Security/Stability.* You need predictable long term stability even if it is at the cost of lack of promotion, excitement and challenge. You are willing to take direction and can live with a degree of boredom and routine. You have a self-effacing style and willingness to be satisfied with modest amounts of change. You are irritated by people who seem to be constantly scrambling for promotion, or by change for change's sake. You judge reward by how far it provides steady, reliable increments with no surprises. You want pleasant working conditions and appreciate benefits in kind such as a pension, health insurance, staff discounts. You judge reward by how far it acknowledges your loyalty and long service.

Points out of ten for how far Security/Stability describes you:

5 *Entrepreneurial Creativity.* Your core need is to create a new business, product or service in your own name and you probably started some kind of trading in childhood.

Business opportunities motivate and stretch you. Your talents are the relentless pursuit of success through hard work, risk-taking with your own capital or effort and being willing to gamble that you are right. You are irritated by bids from others to control you. You judge reward by the extent to which you can retain control. Your own pay may not in itself be an issue unless a high salary also tells the world that you have made it. Promotion as such is irrelevant. You want visible success in the eyes of the world through the value of your company; public attention is welcome.

Points out of ten for how far Entrepreneurial Creativity describes you:

6 *Service/Dedication to a Cause.* Your core need is wanting to do something which improves the world – knowing that you are helping people, a cause, the planet. Your talents are commitment, teamwork and close identification with an organization as long as you can wholeheartedly endorse its aims. You are irritated by organizations which do not practise what they preach. You judge reward by the opportunity it gives to have a bigger influence over the organization's policy and practice. Money is often not a prime motivator. Promotion may not be a motivator at all. You may prefer to stay close to the action with service users because you can see your effectiveness at first hand. The best form of recognition for you is praise from the colleagues you value because they share the same principles as you.

Points out of ten for how far Service/Dedication to a cause describes you:

7 *Pure challenge*. Your core need is conquering the impossible, whether this is a physical, managerial, intellectual or moral challenge. It is important to feel that you are living your life vividly and on the edge. You need to feel you are winning against the odds, to pass daily tests of your own courage. You have a talent for persistence, patience, humour and chutzpah. Pessimists, timidity and monotony irritate you. You judge reward by how far it gives opportunities for further challenge, so conventional promotion is meaningless. If a promotion does not meet the need for single-minded self-testing it will probably be a failure. Your job moves may often have followed an unconventional or unexpected pattern. You want to beat the competition and exceed your own high standards.

Points out of ten for how far Pure Challenge describes you:

8 *Lifestyle*. Your core motivator is integrating your career with your total lifestyle. You need to balance everything in your life: your partner relationship, your children, your personal growth, health, leisure interests, spirituality and your work; to have fun and laughter. You have a talent for relationships, tolerating ambiguity and enjoying yourself. You are irritated by organizations that intrude into personal life and make what seem like unreasonable requests. You judge reward by how far it honours the whole person – for instance, giving opportunities for part-time work, job shares, childcare arrangements, early retirement and so on. Promotion is fine as long as it allows you the flexibility you crave.

Points out of ten for how far Lifestyle describes you:

Ranking the anchors

Now rank your anchors in order of their importance to you. If you have a tie for the top choice: imagine you are forced to choose. Which would you sacrifice last?

Your priority ranking for each career anchor
1
2
3
4
5
6
7
8

Questions to ask:

- How is your number 1 choice reflected in the career moves you have made?
- The core anchor is often reflected in how you live the rest of your life and in other important decisions you have made. Is this true for you? If so, how?
- Your second and third choices often show other important needs in your life. Often these will service your number 1 choice. How true is this for you?
- How does your present or most recent job stack up against your number 1 career anchor?

Completing this exercise can be enlightening as it can reveal exactly why what on the surface was a desirable job turned out to be a poor fit.

Philip, a Medical Director in a large hospital, had been uneasy and unsettled over his well-paid job and was not sorry to lose it as a result of an NHS reorganization. His number 1 anchor was Technical Competence, but his job had required him to be motivated by General Managerial Competence. He had utterly hated the whole business of managerial meetings and manoeuvring with executive team colleagues. He returned thankfully to a role as a senior consultant, working directly with patients and other doctors.

Transferable skills

In making the transition from one job to another, you need to be able to identify what you can offer a new employer – or to reposition your offer to an existing employer. This is less likely to be to do with the context of your existing/old job than with the transferable skills you have developed. The process of finding a new job starts with identifying what those skills are.

When you have made a first pass at this list, it may be worth checking it through with people who know you well. It is often easy to brush aside important skills in a '*doesn't everybody do this well?*' frame of mind, when actually these skills are rare. Even if they are not rare, they will be an important part of what you can offer an employer. Here are some reminders of useful skills – to prompt your own thinking. What specific examples can you identify of places and occasions where you have used them to powerful effect and are proud of what resulted?

Skill	Your examples
Organizing people and events: getting things done, e.g. planning, managing detail, managing projects, staying calm in a crisis	
Physical accomplishments, e.g. manual dexterity, constructing and making things, sport, dealing with equipment	

continued

Skill	Your examples
Analytical and data skills, e.g. entering and checking accuracy of data, managing and retrieving it, numerical skills, seeing trends, thinking strategically	
Problem-solving, e.g. persistence, looking for underlying causes, finding and implementing solutions	
Influencing and persuading, e.g. listening, creating rapport, writing and speaking expressively, resolving conflicts, selling	
Leadership, e.g. inspiring others with a vision, setting high standards, holding people to account, creating loyalty, coaching and developing others	
Managing yourself, self-awareness, e.g. knowing your impact on others, high personal integrity, learning from mistakes, personally well organized	
Creativity, e.g. visual, musical, linguistic, dance abilities or interests; openness to learning; interest in performance	
Customer/client responsiveness, e.g. patience, warmth, flexibility, firmness in dealing with customers, responding promptly and skilfully to requests and complaints	
Teamwork, e.g. loyalty to colleagues, sharing praise and blame, working principally for team not self	
Other	

What does this mean for a future job?

The chances are that when you are working from strengths you will also be enthusiastic – a quality all employers like. As another thought-prompting exercise in this chapter, you might now be able to bring some of this together. The *mind-mapping* technique, developed originally by the writer Tony Buzan in his book *Use Your Head* (latest edition, BBC Active, 2010) is an excellent way to do this because it mimics the way the human brain works. This is that we typically don't think in lists but in ideas where one thought sparks off another. Take another large piece of paper and use this suggested mind map as a way of identifying what you would like your ideal job to be, combining what you know about your personality, career themes so far, emerging interests and skills (see Figure 6.1). It helps to use differently coloured pens for each of the main branches of the diagram – this encourages creativity – adding new branches as you think of further examples and ideas.

Implications

You should now be clearer what your ideal job would be. Being clear does not guarantee you will get it, but should give you a benchmark for measuring any actual job against what you would ideally like. Try now writing yourself a brief statement, completing these phrases:

> An ideal job would be one where I was working with (tools, ideas, puzzles, materials, data . . .)
> in an organization where its purpose was
> using my skills of
> with colleagues who
> which suggests my ideal job is

Putting it all together: your personal 'brand'

In looking for a job you should think of yourself as a brand. You are the product, and just like any other product you will be successful by differentiating yourself from the competition. In most British towns and cities there is a plethora of coffee shops. If you ask people where they buy, most will be able to tell you why they prefer Pret to Costa, or Costa to Caffè Nero or Starbucks – or the Momma and Poppa café off the main road to any of them. It is rarely about price: as customers we are making

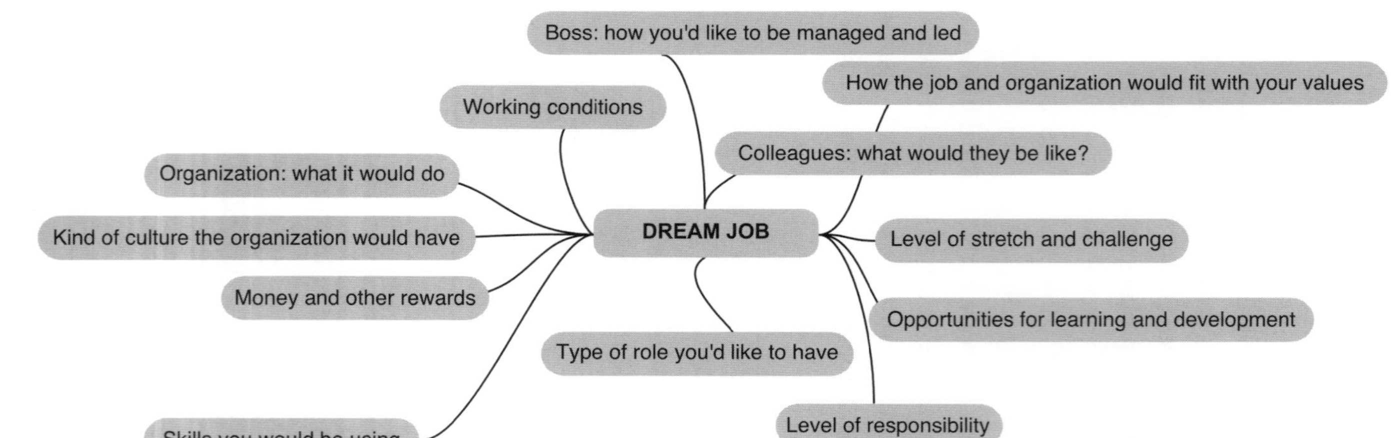

Figure 6.1 Your dream job

fine discriminations between what is essentially the same product – we like the leather chairs, the ever-smiley staff, the extra flavours on offer, the superior croissants, the free Wifi, the company's policy on charitable giving or tax. As a person looking for a new job you need to do the same. Forget ideas about being safe, grey and dull, or too bashful to sing about your strengths. You must differentiate. A brand doesn't need to appeal to everyone. But a successful brand knows who is and is not their target customer, helps us solve a problem and persuades us to part with our money in order to do so, just as an employer will do when they take you onto their staff.

The 'elevator speech'

In starting the active process of job search you really must have a short snappy statement about yourself, your skills and achievements and what you are looking for. Americans call this 'the elevator speech' – the few moments you might have in a lift to answer the question, 'What do you do?' In effect this is a statement of your brand. Work out what to say in advance – don't be left feeling embarrassed with an open mouth and puzzled expression when you are asked the question 'What are you looking for?' Kayleen worked through most of the exercises in this chapter and then prepared her 'brand statement' on paper first:

> I'm a Senior Sister and Intensive Therapy nurse. I've worked with Intensivists, other clinicians, critically ill patients and their families for six years. I was privileged to do part of my training with the Beth Israel Hospital, New York. I'm confident with all aspects of artificial ventilation, sedation and pain management. I hold the Graduate Diploma in Critical Care Nursing from [name of University], pass with Distinction. In my last role I specialized in managing transplant patients and won an award from [name of hospital] for innovative solutions to infection control, reducing infection rates on my

ward by 15%. I have a Diploma in Bereavement Counselling and I'm proud of having been able to give effective help to many families when a dearly loved relative has died. Colleagues, patients and their families consistently tell me I bring humour, a caring attitude and calmness to what can be extremely stressful circumstances. I'm looking now for promotion to [name of role] in an ICU where I can use my skills to the best possible effect.

Kayleen was able to do this because she gave thoughtful answers to the questions below – and you might like to do the same:

Thinking now about what you know about yourself:

What is it that you *do*? What is your work identity?

What distinguishes you from others who seem to do the same thing?

Describe your achievements, the times when you did more than was expected of you

Say what problems you can solve for an employer

Describe what it is like working with you (draw here on positive feedback you have had from former colleagues) and what you bring to a team

Say what you are looking for in a new job

Summary

When you lose a job through redundancy you get the chance to reconsider your career path in the context of your whole life. Often this will prompt questions about what truly brings you fulfilment and helps reconnect with needs which you may have neglected because of a focus on work. Self-awareness is the

foundation for finding a new job and you can increase this through taking psychometric questionnaires, looking at career themes, highlighting your achievements and not being shy about your skills. Having a clear view of yourself as a 'brand' is essential as this will allow you to say clearly what you want in your next job and to differentiate yourself from the competition. This is the necessary first step. Now you have to match this with what your market wants and needs, the subject of the next chapters.

Further reading

What Color is your Parachute? by Richard Nelson Bolles (Ten Speed Press) is an American book updated and republished yearly. It is a comprehensive guide to all aspects of career management, including those in this chapter.

Edgar Schein's pamphlet *Career Anchors Participant Workbook* (Pfeiffer, 2006) is easily ordered online and contains a self-scoring questionnaire to help identify your career anchors, more detailed descriptions of the eight anchors and a helpful discussion of ten typical career stages. The latter half of the book suggests a format for a career review discussion with a partner, as a parallel process to identifying the number 1 Anchor. The brief summary in this chapter is based on this book.

If you are interested in the MBTI and personality, my own book *Sixteen Personality Types at Work in Organizations* gives detailed profiles of each type. It is available through my website: www.JennyRogersCoaching.com.

How to get a Job You'll Love by John Lees, McGraw-Hill Professional 2013–14 edition contains a mass of useful exercises and prompts to understanding who you are and what you want.

7 THINKING BEYOND YOUR TAKEN-FOR-GRANTEDS

Being clear about your ideal job gives you a set of benchmarks for judging any particular path against how far it meets important needs for you. That is one side of the equation. The other is what is going on in the employment market and how you might have to flex what you want against what is actually available: the subject of this chapter.

We can all hold unthinking assumptions about employment. Mostly they are so unthinking that we never question them at all. Being made redundant may bring you sharply up against them and sometimes you need to recognize and then challenge your taken-for-granteds.

Upbringing

It is difficult to overestimate the influence of upbringing on career choice. I have had several clients who are the third or even the fourth generation in their families to go into medicine, the media or the diplomatic service. I have lost count of how many clients who are teachers and academics are the children of people in the same professions. This should not really be surprising as parents and grandparents are powerful role models and you also get to see the daily reality of the life you would be entering. Parents, who themselves feel they have underachieved, may also exert strong pressure on children to enter high-status occupations, such as accountancy or the law.

Ultra-modest expectation can also be passed on. In a village I know well, if you ask young girls how they want to earn a living as adults they will often tell you that they hope to become hairdressers before settling down with babies. The village has meagre transport links, work is mostly seasonal, semi-skilled and poorly paid. Few adults in the village have full-time jobs, so it is not surprising that their children grow up with humble ambitions.

Teachers exert influence too. Some teachers are charismatic, they attract devotion, we want their praise and this can mean that we want to follow their advice or be just like them. But just because you did well at maths does not mean that you should have a career as an accountant or because you wrote a mean history essay that you should do a PhD in history and stay on to teach at the university, or because you got to Grade 8 in piano that you should follow a career as a professional musician.

What we know about other people's jobs can be limited. We know about work where we are customers, so service jobs like sales assistant, taxi driver, hairdresser, caterer or nail technician are easy to understand, as are other jobs where we are clients, such as teacher, accountant, pharmacist, estate agent, optometrist or nurse. But how many people know what a biochemist, food technologist or a business intelligence analyst is, or could say for certain what a structural engineer does?

It is easy for misinformation to be passed on; a lot of it based on rumour and prejudice. Some is based on jealousy – *why should you get a nice job when I didn't, so I'll tread all over your innocent ideas*. Some ideas about work are based on the outmoded and cynical reflections of people who are fixed in the past. So the City is assumed to be full of either 'barrow-boy types' or 'toffs'. Teachers are sometimes alleged to have 'failed' to be good enough to get other work. For a long time people in the public sector assured each other that their pay was cruelly low compared with equivalent jobs in the private sector. None of these stereotypes is true but they can prevent people widening their search for work.

You may think that the media broaden our thinking, but this is questionable. Tabloids seem increasingly preoccupied with celebrity gossip (careers: pop star, actor, footballer, royalty). Television drama and documentaries tend to feature a narrow range of occupations. In descending order these seem to be medicine, nursing, paramedic, police work, chef, lawyer, firefighter, prison officer, with occasional contributions from architects and designers. People who appear as pundits are mostly

journalists, politicians and economists commenting on the work of other journalists, economists and politicians. In soap operas the characters have vaguely sketched in jobs and are rarely seen actually working unless behind a bar or a café counter.

Navigating your way through redundancy to a new job means being prepared to think more broadly and flexibly.

Being realistic about where the work is

In areas of high unemployment, any semi-skilled or unskilled job can attract several hundred applicants. There have been reports recently that a coffee-shop job vacancy in the Midlands attracted over a thousand applicants and a sales assistant job in a furniture store the same number. The applicant base for professional jobs would be smaller, but would still probably mean that the employer might well be tempted just to pick with a pin – indeed many employers in these circumstances will confess privately to only looking at the first dozen or so applicants because to look at them all would be overwhelming.

If this is true for your area, then however painful or difficult it is to contemplate, you might be better off moving away because the competition is just too severe and the impact on self-esteem can be crushing. In the Euro crisis there are countries, for instance Portugal, where net emigration is the norm because it has become the only way to find work, the government actually has an agency which helps people relocate to other countries. Human beings have always been migrants, driven by poverty, war and economic difficulties to change countries in search of a better life.

Duncan is the only person in his family to have any higher education or to leave his home area. Everyone else has stayed put in the Scottish Borders and no one else in his family is economically active. Duncan worked hard for his PhD in mechanical engineering and found a first job in a

Midlands car assembly plant, getting steady promotion. He lost this job when the owners decided to reduce capacity, moving most of the work to Eastern Europe. After a fruitless job search in the UK, very reluctantly, Duncan has decided to accept a job in Canada where there is an opportunity for a design engineer with his experience and skill. He says, 'I'm already the odd one out in my family – they don't get what I do at all, and it's too expensive to go home a lot, but now I'm about to cut myself off even more. I've told myself I'll keep in touch through Skype and I know I'll be miserable and homesick at first, but it's either that or just drift back to the Borders and accept that at 36 my career is over, and I can't do that. I'll be joining the great Scottish Diaspora in Canada and I know there are thousands of people there who've made similarly hard choices'.

Duncan's pragmatic approach is right for him, but these are daunting decisions. Committing to keeping in touch will help, but some people feel that the price to be paid is too high, for instance if it involves a weekly commute, absence from family and a lonely four nights a week in a cheap hotel. It all depends on the circumstances and on a balance of priorities that only you can judge.

Baling out of declining sectors

There's a phenomenon in employment trends known as 'being the last iceman'. What this means is that even when everyone has a refrigerator, there will be a minuscule market for one of the few people left selling ice. You might think you can be that last iceman in your sector, but it is a risk. When the prevailing trend is downwards, it might be better to cut your losses and look elsewhere. In general, sectors in the UK that deal with the extraction of raw materials are suffering most, closely followed by those that turn raw materials into products, (manufacturing), while the people who are doing best are those who sell services, especially IT. But this generalization masks a good deal of variation. Telecoms may be doing well overall but some companies are losing money; construction has been hard hit by recession but some companies are thriving. Do your research and take a measured view. If you have been working in a declining sector, it is likely that all your company's competitors will also be suffering so the chances of finding a comparable job are probably slim. Look at what is flourishing and growing – and where, including internationally.

Being flexible

Sometimes I work with clients who are clear what they want from a new job, but perhaps they are too clear because what they want is not always compatible with what is actually available.

David wanted a strategy job with a London-based think tank that was an exact match with his right-leaning political views and he also wanted to work only three days a week in order to pursue a degree in Art History.

Sharon was a child psychiatrist and sought a consultant post within a relatively small radius of Bristol and which would allow her to devote a large percentage of her time to continuing her research into autism, to teaching medical students and to doing a minimal number of hours with actual patients.

Roxanne wanted to improve on the relatively low salary she received as an Events Manager specializing in a particular type of scientific conference and to do roughly the same role as before. She disliked being away from home.

As shopping lists for a new job, these were fine for starters, but they all contained too many irreconcilable elements. David had to compromise on the exactness of the match with his political views as well as working four not three days a week; Sharon either had to agree to spending more of her time with patients or to broadening her geographical radius, and Roxanne's previous salary proved to be the industry norm; to earn more she had to go freelance and be prepared to travel, as the growth market for her type of event is in Africa. Starting by demanding particular hours or conditions also gives employers a reason to exclude you at an early stage. It is better to be offered the job and then to negotiate.

Sometimes you may also need to be flexible about conditions and culture when considering any possible new job. The longer we stay in one organization, the more blind we become to its funny little ways. It can be a shock to move to an organization where there are different assumptions about working hours, environment, attitudes to conflict, hierarchy and many others.

> *My previous organization had been frankly a bit sleepy. We took an hour off for lunch, went out for a walk or did shopping, finished at 5 on the dot. In the new job people eat sandwiches at their desks and you only leave when the work is done. I don't mind – in fact I quite like it; I feel more alert and as if what I'm doing matters.*
>
> *In the old job I'd had a lot of freedom. I've had to come to terms with a far more regimented and controlling regime. I'm putting up with it for now because it's a job and I need it, but I don't think I'll stay long.*

Being prepared to consider new patterns of employment

There is more about this in Chapter 11, but working patterns have changed and continue to do so. Rather than thinking that you must have a full-time job with a continuing contract, it

might be better to consider an offer that at least puts you back on the employment ladder.

Rob was made redundant from his job in a retail bank. He was offered a six-month secondment in another section of the bank and saw it as a way of broadening his experience. While there, he made a good friend of an external consultant, a specialist in customer relations management (CRM), who set up an interview with the boss of his firm. Rob was offered a temporary contract which he accepted, seeing it as a route to a new career as a CRM specialist himself.

Sophie had worked in the billing department of a fulfilment house. There were no other jobs exactly like it to be had, but she found two part-time roles which in different ways played to her strengths in handling difficult customers and dealing with money.

Jonno had always loved cars with a natural talent for repairs and maintenance, so when his job with a house-building company disappeared he decided to make a radical break, blagged his way into a car repair centre owned by two friends of his Dad's where he did three days a week, put himself on a specialist computer-diagnostics training course and developed a thriving small business on eBay selling cheap copies of designer watches in whatever time was left.

A temporary job can lead to a permanent one. A secondment gives an employer the chance to see if they like you and you the chance to see if you like them. Short-term contracts in unfamiliar territory can provide low-risk ways of trying out a new sector and new type of job. No job is a life sentence. You can always leave and start again if you discover that you hate it.

Being prepared to consider different types of employer

This can be a challenge for people who have been committed for many years to public sector work. It is not chance that they have been in public sector employment – they believe that services such as health should be free at the point of contact. They loathe the individualistic attitudes which reward what they see as selfish behaviour; they understand that in a mature society you must look after the weak as well as rewarding the strong. They believe they can see for themselves, thanks to some well publicized private sector failures (G4S at the 2012 Olympic Games is just one spectacular example) that the private sector is not necessarily the home of greater efficiency. But with public sector organizations having their monopoly contracts removed, many such employees are being forced to think again. In deciding whether or not to bid for such work, it is important to distinguish myth and prejudice from reality. Ask yourself:

What values does this company say it espouses?

What reputation does the part of it have that I might join?

Who do I know who works there and who might give me reliable information?

Who owns the company? What is their record on human rights, equality, charitable donation?

What would the actual work be? What would I be expected to deliver?

Sometimes the difference between the old and new worlds can be too small to matter, yet people can get stuck on the apparent clashes.

Aidan had been a senior manager in the NHS but lost his job as a result of reorganization. He was soon offered a job running a small hospital for a private healthcare company.

He dithered for so long about whether this squared with his public sector values that the offer was withdrawn. As his coach I had pointed out to him that the healthcare company was a 'mutual', so not a profit-making concern and was also carrying out a great deal of work for NHS patients. But this did not seem to matter and a year later Aidan was still unemployed and was bitterly regretting that he had not accepted the one offer that had been made to him.

Think small companies

It is easy to get fixed into thinking that it is only ever worth considering large employers because these are the organizations that get all the attention. But the fact is that there are far more small rather than large organizations. Mostly a small organization will be less hidebound by rules and more prepared to think flexibly. They can be approached more informally and it is far easier to find out who to target with a speculative letter (see Chapter 8). Roles will tend to be less specialized and, once in the job, there may be more chance to show what you can do. The disadvantage is that career progression is often limited, but so what? By the time this becomes a reality you will be ready to move on again and with luck you will have additional skills and experience to offer to another company.

Being realistic about salary

There is a delicate path to tread here. If you compromise too soon you may regret it. If you are too fixed on reproducing or exceeding the salary that you had before being made redundant, you may miss opportunities to get back into work. This is an especial difficulty for people whose previous jobs have been in declining sectors. Their salaries have often been high, set in better times when their company was in better shape. It can be challenging to acknowledge that by current standards they were overpaid. Some serious self-questioning will probably suggest the solution, plus consulting recruiters in your field, as they have nothing to gain from lying to you:

How easily will my skills transfer?

What is the going rate for similar jobs in parallel sectors?

Given my age, experience and skills, how easy or difficult is it going to be to get a job that pays the same or more?

Sometimes the answers will be positive and there will be every reason to hold out for a well paid job. For other people it will be better to compromise. Never get exaggeratedly fixed on some symbolic sum – for instance by telling yourself that you if you don't earn £40,000 you will lose every shred of self-esteem. If you are offered a job at £38,995, after tax there will be very little difference to the money in your pocket. Occasionally I have seen clients decide to make radical compromises.

Sean, who had earned over £250,000 in a very senior role in his previous job, but in a sector in rapid decline, realized after 14 months of unemployment that it was more important to him to have a job of any sort than to languish at home. He was 52 and felt time was running out. He took a job in a not-for-profit organization and a sector totally new to him which paid a fraction of his previous salary, telling himself that the work was worthwhile, would be testing, enjoyable and would involve new learning. Two years later he had added another 30% to his salary through sheer determination and talent, and was poised to make another move to an even better paid job in his new sector. His own view is matter of fact: 'I was lucky to be paid so much before and now I feel lucky again to have been given another chance. In effect I am living proof that a second career can be even more rewarding than the first, though in this case, not financially!'

Similarly it doesn't do to get too caught up on job titles. A client who had been looking for a job for eight months was at last offered something which paid slightly more than she had been earning previously and ticked all her boxes for interest and enjoyment, but did not have the word *Senior* in the job title. She felt this was a grievous affront to her sense of status and considered turning it down. Fortunately she soon saw that this would not have been sensible. Job titles vary hugely between organizations, have little meaning beyond them and rarely have much to do with the actual authority that goes with the job.

Research is the answer

The simplest answer to all of the dilemmas in this chapter is to commit to doing your research. Notice any tendency to think in stereotyped ways about employment opportunities, whether this is about sectors, reward or types of job. Make it your business to extend the range of jobs with which you are familiar and don't rule anything out before you have investigated it and prised the facts away from emotion and prejudice. Research is a critically important part of job-searching – the subject of the next chapter.

Summary

It is easy to think too narrowly about careers and jobs since we are all affected by opinions from our families, teachers, the media and friends. But with work changing as fast as it is, you cannot afford to be too restrictive in your thinking. It is worth considering relocating, revising your salary expectations if necessary, looking at small companies as well as large ones and assessing coolly where you might find another job even if the conditions are different from everything you have experienced so far in your career.

Further reading

Any book about the state of the employment market is likely to become out of date quickly. A better guide is to become a regular reader of the business pages in broadsheet newspapers or in magazines such as *The Economist*.

8 JOB SEARCH: WHAT REALLY WORKS

The main reason that people find it difficult to get new jobs is that their assumptions and beliefs about what works are not consistent with how it really happens. It would be common, for instance, for disillusioned job seekers to describe sending out literally hundreds of CVs with little or no acknowledgement. I know of one job seeker who stood outside a conference hall handing out her CV, and of another who toured all the shops in his high street doing the same. Others apply for multiple jobs online. None of these tactics is likely to land a job and the disillusioned job seeker concludes that all employers are heartless exploiters of the weak.

Myths about finding a job

The mismatch between expectations and reality could not be more stark. The inexperienced job seeker believes all of this to be true:

Most jobs are advertised.

The process is open and transparent, based on objective facts.

Employers read unsolicited CVs carefully.

Formal qualifications are what matter.

The employer will approach you if they can see that you are experienced.

Your past experience should speak for itself.

Old boy networks make it impossible for anyone else to get a look in.

It's wrong to sell yourself too hard to an employer.

The employer is interested in you.

All of these are myths. The main way employers fill jobs is through internal promotions, many of which may not be advertised, even internally. After that they appoint other people they know, either through personal networks or through a recommendation from a colleague. If none of this turns up a suitable candidate, they may take on a recruitment agency they trust because this agency has found the right candidate in the past. If still stuck, they will, extremely reluctantly, advertise. If very, very stuck, they may comb through a carelessly assembled pile of CVs.

The reason the market works this way is that employers always prefer to hire someone who is a known quantity, and this makes perfect sense because it reduces risk. Employers are not interested in you, though they may pretend that they are. They want you to be interested in them. Their only concern is in solving the problem that a vacancy has created. They don't read CVs that are sent to them on spec and they hate spending money on finding a new employee. At the selection stage, even though this may be garlanded with tests, pomp and checklists, the decision is more likely to be made on hunch than on anything objectively fair.

If this seems tough, take heart. You can hugely elevate your chances of getting a job by playing employers at their own game. There are two rules here, the number one rule of which is: TARGET and the number two rule is TAKE THE INITIATIVE. Essentially you have to see the whole job search process from the employer's perspective, not yours, identifying what you *offer* them not what you *want* from them. If you sit at home waiting for the employer to discover your unique gifts, you will wait for ever. This is also why it pays to have given careful thought to what you want, your skills and your ideal organization and job, as discussed in the previous chapters, because then you will not be wasting time courting employers who are not a good fit with you nor you with them.

A strategic plan

Another mistake that inexperienced job seekers make is to over-rely on one method of finding a job. Typically this would be

either sending out a CV or waiting for the right advertisement to appear. They then believe in hedging their bets by applying for anything that seems even vaguely right: a tactic that is guaranteed to fail. You can shorten the speed and effectiveness of a job search dramatically if you make yourself a strategic plan. So your overall strategy might be 'Find a job as X at a salary of Y in Z type of organization by [date]'. To do this you will need to deploy as many channels of searching as possible, so the canny job seeker uses multiple approaches: personal contacts (networking), targeted speculative letters, responding to ads, making shrewd use of recruiters, making social media work for you, online searches, volunteer, part-time and interim projects.

Networking

The better your networking, the quicker and easier it will be to find a new job. Networking has a bleak reputation. If you ask people how they feel about it they will often screw up their faces with distaste. It has come to mean self-serving overconfidence and fake friendliness where the aim is to *exploit* others. This is not true networking. In fact we all network naturally – for instance when we ask friends whom they would recommend as a GP, who cuts their hair or what secondary school their child attends. I prefer the idea of what I call *generous networking* where the whole process is reciprocal: you give as much as you get. Your network is like a bank specializing in favours where you have credits and debits and it works on the understanding that even when you are looking for a favour you may have something you can offer in return. Networking is only difficult if you see yourself as a petitioner who could be rejected, even more so if you believe it is the social equivalent of cold-calling.

Networking – and luck

The better connected you are – that is the more effectively you network – the luckier you are likely to consider yourself to

be. And maybe the luckier you actually are can matter a lot in job search where, as in most situations, we largely make our own luck. This is because with an extensive network, you are more likely to have people to turn to when something goes wrong, to ask for and get support and to be able to float ideas with others, and make 'lucky' chance encounters. You will learn about new trends in your areas of interest, get early warning of new jobs and get helpful feedback about yourself.

How do you tell if you have a large enough network?

One study run by Hertfordshire University correlated luckiness with how many people you know on first name terms from each of 15 surnames. In this study, 65% of people knew someone with the most common name, Wilson, versus only 15% who knew someone with the least common name on the list, Byrne. People who did not consider themselves either lucky or unlucky scored on average 6. Lucky people scored 8 or more and unlucky people 5 or fewer. Only 8 of the 4,000 people who took part claimed to know someone with all 15 names.[1]

Charting your network

Take as big a piece of paper as you can find – if you have access to a flip chart that would be ideal. You are going to map your network and probably surprise yourself by how big it is. If you completed the support chart on page 66 this will also be a useful prompt to your thinking. Use the circles on Figure 8.1 to prompt your thinking and draw further circles if sub-groups occur to you, scribbling down the names of

1 How many do you know? (Alternative spellings of the same name allowed.) Names are in order of most to least common: Wilson, Williams, Walker, Thomas, Taylor, Scott, Ryan, Roberts, Reid, Moore, Hughes, Davies, Campbell, Baker, Byrne.

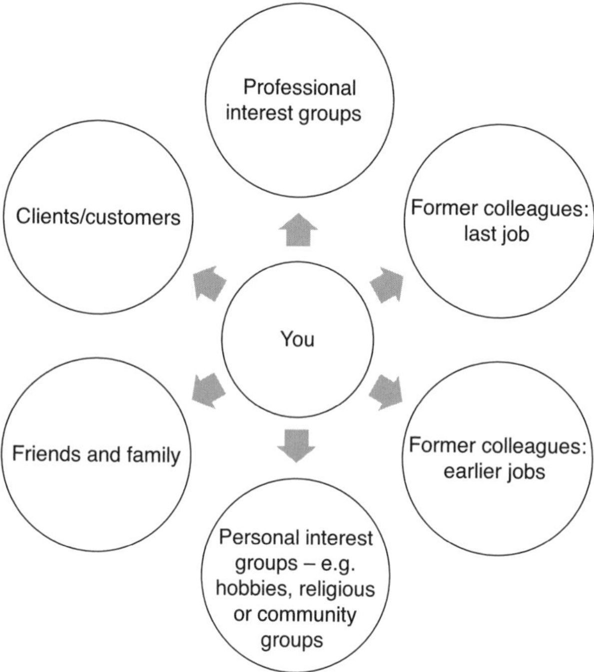

Figure 8.1 Your network

individuals. Over the next few days, keep returning to it to add names.

Charting a network is about assessing who might be able to help you. It is a first step to finding a job. You are alerting your network to what you need and this may take any number of forms, from books you might read, Internet sites you might search, email addresses of influential managers, offers to critique your CV as well as people who might eventually lead you to the person who offers you a job. Networking is not, repeat not, on its own a way to get an actual job.

When you believe you have exhausted the number of names you can think of, remind yourself of the preparatory work you have done on getting clarity about what you want and can offer. Now scan your network chart carefully and star people who might be able to assist you.

Lauren realized that her father had a friend who worked in a nationally known law practice, one of her target markets for a trainee solicitor role after being made redundant from a small practice as a paralegal

After losing his job in the probation service, Matthew realized he had a lot to offer as a manager of services aimed at young offenders. He dug out the participant list he had kept from a major conference, including those from providers of security services such as Serco and G4S, remembering the people he had spoken to while there.

Get yourself a business card

A business card is the simplest possible tool and investment for this part of your job search campaign. It is as much a part of the ritual of business communication as is shaking hands. Give it to contacts either immediately on meeting them or at the end of the conversation. All it needs is your name and contact details, printed simply and elegantly on good quality card. Any local stationary franchise or shop will be able to print 200 cards, using one of a range of standard designs, cheaply and quickly.

Research interviews

Research interviews are one of the best ways of finding a new job. When you deploy this approach you are serving several purposes at once. You are growing your understanding of your target employment market, you are acting as PR agent for your personal brand, you are letting people know what it is you are looking for and you are expanding that precious network.

How it works is that you call or email your contact, mentioning how you know them and making sure to mention the name of

the mutual acquaintance who may have given you their details. This first stage is about setting up a time for the interview itself. Say you will need about 20–30 minutes and that it can be done on the phone or face to face. Always opt for face to face if you get the opportunity as this will give you a better chance to make an impression. Explain that you are looking for advice on opportunities in their field/organization/profession.

The focus in the conversation is on them not on you. Remember that this is not a selling conversation: you are not there to ask for a job. Start by reconfirming what the purpose of your conversation is, i.e. to get information and to get referrals. Re-check that your interviewee still has time to talk to you and promise them that you will stick to your allotted 20 (or 30) minutes. Your questions are about uncovering what the employment trends are in their organization or sector, which types of job are growing, which shrinking, how people typically get those jobs and what kind of experience is looked for. While you are doing this you are listening carefully for matches to your own needs and experience.

About 8 minutes from the end of your promised 20–30 minutes, you deliver your 'elevator speech' (page 123) and then say: 'What advice would you give me about the next steps in my job search?' The most common responses are practical suggestions about getting more experience of a particular type, consulting a website, and most pricelessly valuable of all, another person to contact. If such a name is not offered, ask, 'Who else do you think I should talk to?' swiftly followed by, 'May I mention your name?' Permission to mention the name matters because it will ensure that the next person will not wish to offend your present contact by refusing to talk to you.

Follow up with a brief, pleasant email or letter, thanking the person enthusiastically for their time and advice. If they have asked to see your CV, this is the time to send it.

Setting up a spread sheet

At first it is easy to keep track of who you are seeing and how you promised to follow up or keep in touch. As the process becomes more complicated, it is easy to drift and to forget who said what. Four or five headings are usually enough: person's name including notes about their preferences and lifestyle, contact details, organization, when last seen, next steps.

Speculative letters

You can waste a lot of time writing emails and speculative letters whose only destination is the trash folder or the waste bin. This will be because the writer has made one or more of these mistakes: the recipient's or company's name is wrongly spelt; it is clear that it is a mass mailing; the letter is addressed to the wrong person (that busy chief executive will most certainly not have time to read a letter from someone asking for a middle-level position). Other mistakes are to write in a cringingly apologetic style where the first sentence is 'Unfortunately I was made redundant in . . .' or it is over-personal (e.g. addressing a complete stranger too informally); it is written in an hysterical or over-pert style with triple exclamation marks and too many capital letters; it has spelling, grammar and punctuation mistakes; it is vague and all about the job seeker with nothing about the organization.

Speculative letters can work well: as long as they are closely targeted and carefully written. This means that your networking conversations have suggested where there might be vacancies. An Internet search reveals more information about the organization and the name of the probable hiring manager. You do further research on this person, for instance looking at their LinkedIn profile and Twitter feeds. You double-check their job title and how they spell their name.

You deliberately do not send a CV with a speculative letter – it represents a first point of contact and its aim is to get you in

front of the hiring boss where, if all goes well, you can take it to the next stage: a CV followed by an informal interview.

The format

A paper letter in a classic typeface sent on good quality A4 plain white or cream paper in a matching envelope is better than email because it will have more impact. The tone is confident and friendly without being over-chatty. This is a formal letter so their address goes into the left-hand side of the letter immediately below your address and all your contact details.

You begin formally with Dear Mr/Mrs/Ms/Dr/Professor because you don't know them

1st para: about 35 words, states that you are contacting them because you believe you have skills and experience in [you name the job and field] that they might need. You mention the mutual acquaintance who has suggested that you get in touch.

2nd para: about 50 words, says what you admire about their department or organization, their values and achievements – this reflects the research you have done into what they do and how they do it.

3rd para: about 75 words, based again on your research, describes what problems you think you might be able to solve for them, how you might contribute and gives the highlights of your career and experience.

4th para: about 40 words, says that if all of the above is interesting you would like to send a full CV and arrange a face to face meeting. You will call them to see when it is possible to arrange this.

Sign off with 'Yours sincerely' and with a handwritten signature above the typed one.

Never expect the recipient to contact you – remember the rule about always taking the initiative. It is your role to make the next move and to remain true to your promise in the letter that you will contact them. If you are turned away, then this tells you that your research could be faulty and this is not your job or organization. More usually, even if the answer is 'No, not at the moment' the chances are that you will have made a good impression and will have created a new contact to add to your network and spreadsheet.

Using social media and the Internet

Social media have transformed communication and they can transform your job search. What kind of Internet presence do you have? Ask a friend who is prepared to be candid to search your name on Google and to tell you what impression this gives. It may be that you have opted for privacy and have little or no presence. The plus of this tactic is that there is little to conclude about you, so an employer would have to form their impressions from how you actually present to them. The minus is that it leads people to fantasize, not always positively, about the reasons for your invisibility. Are you an Internet-phobe? Are you afraid of technology? Are you one of those people who boasts about not having a computer? Are you a lurker on Twitter (have an account but never tweet)? Do you have something to hide?

When you are a strong candidate all employers will do an Internet search on you, so you need to make sure that nothing they come up with could embarrass you. Rather, it should enhance what they already know. As with all other aspects of looking for a new job, everything you do should reflect the thinking you have done on your personal brand. So if your Facebook account has no privacy controls and allows any visitor, including a prospective employer, to see indiscreet photographs of your clubbing adventures plus inane chatter with your friends, this will not be a recommendation. If your

Twitter account is a would-be amusing avatar who vents wild opinions on current events, this may be at odds with the impression you are trying to create of wisdom and sobriety. Because it is so temptingly simple to tweet, wherever you are from a phone or tablet, social media encourage unconsidered idiocy and can stay around to haunt you, even after you have deleted something banal, silly or offensive. All the other principles of networking apply to social media, so see it as an opportunity to share good practice, interesting articles and videos.

Facebook is probably most useful for letting your friends and family know about your job search, asking them to send you suggestions about people you might contact. You should protect your privacy by going to the Account drop-down menu, choosing Edit Friends, adding the names of anyone where you want to limit access. In the same menu you can choose Customize Settings. This gives various options for limiting access.

LinkedIn is the best professional network. First, go back to your network chart and send everyone on it an invitation to join your network if they are not already a LinkedIn connection. Whenever you meet a new person who might make a mutually useful contact, check them on LinkedIn and send them an invite. Make sure that you have a brief up-to-date CV, a professionally taken photograph and that your profile says what kind of job you are looking for (page 121). Ask people for recommendations, as this will bring your profile to life – what other people say about us is always more convincing than what we say about ourselves.

Use LinkedIn's message facility to send everyone in your network an email about your current situation, asking for suggestions and advice. Update your page at least fortnightly as this will prompt LinkedIn to send status updates to all your connections. The site will send you lists of vacancies posted by employers, another reason for being as specific as possible about your own profile. You can also use LinkedIn to search a target company and the people in it who seem to be promising connections. LinkedIn gives you a place to write a headline, so use this to convey a specific impression, avoiding vague words like 'Consultant', 'Teacher' or 'Marketing Professional'. The site will list people you know through shared connections and one click will send them an invitation to join your network, and the site will also suggest interest groups that you might join. Joining at least three sector-related interest groups will extend your reach and keep you in touch with developments in your field.

Twitter: the art here is frequent posts but again it's about consistency with your brand. You may want to set up a separate account specifically devoted to your job search, letting followers see how the story is unfolding and asking people to re-tweet your posts. You can also use Twitter to search, so if you visit www.search.twitter.com you can click on the Advanced Search menu and enter *hiring* and *jobs* in the first field. Add your postcode and radius in the Places section. You can also refine your search by adding specific job names. Where an employer looks interesting, add them to your Follow list as this will keep you up to date with current developments. Re-tweet anything that you think might interest your followers including links that others have posted. To find new sources of interesting links, join www.StumbleUpon.com which will send you high-quality links to material which reflect your interests and which you can then send to your followers.

Tweeting the main company account is largely a waste of time for several reasons. First, these accounts are handled by the marketing department, not by HR. Secondly, in only 140 characters you are unlikely to be able to say anything compelling about yourself. It is far better to follow up research interviews (page 148) with tweets to individuals. As ever, the best way to impress a recruiter is to come as a recommendation from a source they trust.

There are many *job boards* out there but my experience with clients is that job boards are a lot more useful for tracking down jobs than they are for encouraging employers to find you. Most have local sites and will encourage job-alerts where you get early notice of available jobs. It may also be worth visiting www.glassdoor.com for frank views on an organization you are considering working for as well as for updates on local vacancies. Large employers usually have a vacancies tab on their websites so, once you have decided that this employer might be a promising place to look for work, it will be worth visiting the website frequently.

Blogging is an easy way to show prospective employers what you can offer. You can link a blog with Twitter, Facebook and LinkedIn accounts. With www.wordpress.com you can start a free blog account and can choose from a number of ready-made graphic formats. The blog can be about your job search, or more usefully, can be a platform for insightful opinions and suggestions about trends in your profession or sector. Adding links to other sites and articles will tell a prospective employer a lot about who you are and what interests you, so as with all social media it is essential to weigh what you write and to pay attention to grammar and spelling.

Nine steps to getting a job

Be patient. Finding a job is no different from most other kinds of selling where a high-value product – in this case you – is the focus. It would be very rare indeed for an employer to meet you for the first time and then impulsively offer you a job. Experienced salespeople know that most sales involve up to nine contacts or steps, sometimes more. Typically in job search these might be:

1. Make contact to set up a research interview.
2. Do the research interview.

3. Follow up with an email or tweet.
4. Send a follow up CV.
5. Phone call to explore a possible job.
6. Meet informally face to face to discuss a possible vacancy.
7. Meet more formally for a selection interview.
8. Negotiate terms by phone.
9. Sign the contract.

Managing your time when you are unemployed

At first the free time that unemployment creates can be welcome. No more scrambling to get dressed in the mornings, no need for working weekends and out-of-hours phone calls. The opportunity to reflect is enjoyable. But after a bit the freedom can become oppressive, you miss the structure of the working day and week. Anxiety about getting another job can produce paralysis rather than productivity, leading to a severe dip in self-confidence.

You can avert this danger in a number of ways. Having a strategy and acting on it is the foundation, as is devoting a planned amount of time daily to the whole task of finding another job.

My client Leigh had been 25 years in the same pharmaceutical company when he was unexpectedly made redundant. He says, 'At first it was awful, I felt my daily clock was still set to work as frantically as I had before, I felt purposeless and adrift. But I soon realized that my energy was an asset that I could sweat. I mapped my network just as you recommended, set up a spreadsheet and spent 2 hours every day at the computer emailing recruiters, friends, posting tweets, searching job sites. I also used my support group (page 67) ruthlessly even though I was a bit afraid they would get tired of me. My policy was to have at least three face-to-face meetings a week over coffee or a drink and two research interviews. Then I would email those people to thank them.

It really paid off. It took six months, but the job I got was through one of those face-to-face contacts and it was an introduction to a well-known firm of lobbyists who needed someone just like me with a Big Pharma background to act as go-between with governments. The job was actually created for me'.

Volunteering

Any employer will want to know how you have been using your time after losing your job. Apart from interim and consultancy work (see Chapter 11) the other valuable tactic is to offer yourself as a volunteer. Your choice could be to do something which is recognizably in your professional sphere, so an accountant might offer to be treasurer of a local society, a teacher might mentor school students, or you might choose something totally different.

Douglas had been a senior economist when his consulting firm went under. While he was looking for a new job he set up a football coaching scheme for 5- to 8-year-olds in his village even though he was not much of a player himself. His thinking was that it was a good way of acquiring coaching skills as well as enabling him to stay fit and to enjoy the company of his own 6-year-old.

Charlotte, an IT specialist, deliberately decided not to make herself available for the kind of volunteer work which had anything to do with IT, and chose instead to join a visiting scheme for housebound and disabled single people in her London borough, something which stretched and energized her as it was so unlike anything she had ever done before.

Volunteer roles are well worth any effort they cost you. Most employers approve of people who can think beyond immediate self-interest, as the chances are that this is the kind of person who will do the same at work. It shows initiative and persistence; it is also yet another way of making valuable connections.

Joanne joined a local conservation group as she had always been interested in ecology and had in depth expertise and qualifications as a plantswoman. 'I was hard at work at our bi-annual weekend of rubbish-clearing on the local towpath and got into conversation with another of the volunteers. He told me about a new project in one of the parks where he works. I took the name of the person to contact, was on the phone the next Monday, got an interview, got a six-month temporary contract and then when a wonderful vacancy came up, got made permanent!'

When you volunteer it gives you a purpose which is about service to others and is therefore a bulwark against self-pity. It is a way to keep your skills fresh and can be an excellent addition to the evidence section on your CV. Volunteering keeps you grounded, whether you are unemployed or not. My own shifts at Margins (unionchapel.org.uk/pages/margins), relentlessly hard physical graft, where we feed 150 marginalized local people every Sunday, is a constant reminder of my own luck and of how fragile the line can be between success and failure – 'there but for the grace of God . . .'.

Looking after yourself

A period of unemployment can be an opportunity to get into shape with a regime of prudent eating and exercise. What we eat has a profound effect on how we feel: eat junk, feel like junk. The rules of healthy eating are simple and you will already know

what they are: cut out sugar of all sorts (fizzy drinks, sweets, cakes, biscuits, fruit drinks), reduce saturated fats and salt, eat some lean protein at every meal, eat eight or nine portions of fruit and vegetables every day, limit alcohol. Get enough sleep. Exercise keeps you looking and feeling fit and does not need to be violent, in fact recent research shows that walking briskly every day has more beneficial impact on cardiovascular health than running. There is also research demonstrating that exercise is as good as, or possibly better than, medication for mild depression and with none of the side effects.

Training

Sometimes the result of pondering where your life and career is going is that you decide you want to change direction, or maybe that you want to develop new leisure interests. If so, a period of unemployment is a good time to get additional training and the offer to pay for it may be part of your leaving package. My clients have taken a wide variety of opportunities here which have included an intensive Spanish language course, learning how to design websites, touch typing, teacher training, textile construction, plumbing, full scale degree courses - and many more.

Summary

The most successful strategies involve multiple ways of looking for a job. A targeted approach to specific employers works far better than just sending out an unsolicited CV. Mapping a network of contacts, logging them and then using research interviews, carefully composed speculative letters and social media can all work as a way of getting in front of an employer. Volunteer work is one of the best ways of keeping skills and morale up. Looking after your physical health with a sensible eating and exercise regime is hugely beneficial and getting additional training can extend your interests and skills.

Further reading

How to get a Job you'll Love, by John Lees (McGraw-Hill Professional, 2013–14 edition) contains a detailed guide to managing research interviews (on page 290).

Don't Send A CV by Jeffrey J. Fox (Vermilion, 2009) is a short, bracing book packed with excellent advice about job-searching.

Job Searching with Social Media for Dummies (Wiley, 2011), by Joshua Waldman, gives up-to-date and incisive advice on how to use social media skilfully as part of job-searching.

9 POWERFUL CVS

In this chapter I look at where CVs help in the search for a new job and suggest some ideas on how to make yours stand out for its excellence.

The role of CVs in job search

Think of a CV as a piece of advertising copy. Like any advertising copy its purpose is to create interest in the product, which in this case is you, and like any advert it can instantly turn people off if it is clumsily devised, or it can intrigue and invite more exploration when skilfully presented. The CV does not get you the job: when closely targeted it gets you on the shortlist or into a boss's office for an interview. No one has ever got a job on the basis of their CV alone. When you send a CV in response to an advertisement the average amount of time the reader devotes to a first scrutiny is likely to be less than 30 seconds. The more applications there are, the less time that harassed scrutineer will give.

Always tailor the CV for a particular reader. It will be immediately obvious if you are sending an all-purpose CV and this will tell a potential employer for certain that you have not bothered to research what they need or maybe even to read the job description. Nothing annoys employers more.

> *I advertised for a PA and had applications from people so wildly unsuitable it was comical – included a former refuse collector and someone who said she couldn't type but could learn quickly!*
>
> *We state what experience is essential, for instance must have worked in a Spanish-speaking Latin American country and have fluent Spanish, but you'd never know this is what we asked for when you read so many of the CVs. They barely seem to have glanced at the job pack – do they really think we're that desperate – or just stupid?*

First impressions

Over the years I have been working as a coach it is possible that I have seen about a thousand CVs. Roughly three-quarters fail the first impression test. One client showed me a CV which was so long, at 35 pages, that it was beautifully bound and had its own table of contents. When challenged he was mystified and hurt: 'but this IS my career' he said, unable at first to see that what was fascinating and important to him would give the impression of self-obsession and wordiness to anyone who did not know the pleasant, modest and talented man he actually was. Many people have heard the advice about keeping to two pages, but they cheat by squeezing the margins to a few miserable millimetres and then make it worse by choosing a tiny typeface with single spacing. How does this look? Horrible: do you really want to seem as cramped and mean as that page? Others decide to let their inner artist loose and go for a fanciful and difficult-to-read typeface such as Lucida Calligraphy or over-decorate the page with shaded boxes, many different type sizes, italic, inserted objects, gaudy colour, bullets and underlines.

Style and layout

A good first impression is made by a CV that is simple, elegant and therefore easy to read. Stick to the Word default of 2.54cm top, bottom and side margins and never go smaller than 11 point. Use a classic typeface such as Times New Roman, Calibri, Gill Sans or Trebuchet. Typeface size 12 point is ideal. A serif typeface (has little hooks on the letters) is easier to read than a sans serif typeface such as Arial.

Select the whole document, choose single-line spacing and then use the paragraph menu on your computer and choose *6pt Before* to give a pleasing amount of white space between paragraphs, not too much and not too little. Left-justify is safer than justifying both sides as this will avoid strange white spaces appearing on the page. Stick to bold in the same size typeface for headings. Too many boxes looks messy. Don't overuse bullets: no more than eight per page is a safe rule. Underline is unnecessary when you can create the same effect in a more uncluttered way with bold. You don't need to have Curriculum Vitae in huge letters at the top of page 1, but you do need to have *CV/your name* and the page number in small type as a footer so that if your CV is printed off by the receiver and one page becomes detached from the rest, it will be easy to retrieve.

Double-check grammar, spelling and punctuation. An amazing number of people do not know the rules, so for instance the frequent misuse of apostrophes seems to be getting worse. I saw *Coconu'ts'* on a market stall recently, an even more bizarre mistake than adding unnecessary apostrophes to simple plurals. Make sure you are not misspelling words like definite, necessary, accommodate and separate, four of the 30 English words that people most commonly get wrong. A great many jobs involve writing, so if your CV contains these kinds of errors, some detail-conscious grammarian will most probably spot them and you will have ruled yourself out straight away as 'uneducated' or 'sloppy'.

If your first draft CV maunders on for three or more pages in 10 pt type, then the solution is to minimize the words not the typeface. Anything more than 800 words long is too long and 600 words is better. Two pages is the limit.

Why that first page is so important

Remember that the employer is busy and preoccupied. They don't want to wait until the bottom of page 2 to find out why you are such a good fit for them. If the first page does not grab their attention it is likely that they will never get to the second page. I see many strong candidates throw their chances away by filling their first page with a sprawling address in huge type, followed by their qualifications triple-spaced, then by all the many training courses they have attended. None of this interests the employer.[2] Employers like to see a Profile/Career Summary as the first paragraph and then they want to know how your skills and achievements meet their needs, either with a succinct outline of how you have made a difference in your current role or with a skills summary.

Writing the profile paragraph

Profile or summary paragraphs as the first part of the CV come in and out of fashion. At the moment they are in fashion. Regardless of fashion, a profile paragraph is a sound idea as it gives an employer two vital clues about whether or not they should invite you for interview: it tells the employer how you see yourself and it is a crisp guide to what follows in the rest of the CV.

There is an art in writing a summary profile. First, please avoid stating the obvious or the clichéd, so ban words like *professional, experienced, dynamic, results-oriented, self-motivated, team-player, enthusiastic*. If you do not have those qualities then you are a non-starter anyway. Go back to the work you did on your personal brand (page 121), remembering that the art in job-seeking is to differentiate yourself. Highlight the key words and now do the same with the employer's job description including anything such as qualifications that they mention as essential. These are the words that should appear in your profile summary. Here is the formula:

2 The exception is that for jobs where licensing is involved, such as nursing or the law, you should give your reference details and qualifications on the first page and these employers usually ask for evidence of Continuing Professional Development as this is mandatory.

The total word count should be under 100.

1. Name the role or job and say how many years of experience you have in it, mentioning any essential qualifications. The name you give your job should as near as possible be the name of the job vacancy that the employer wants to fill.
2. Describe the context in which you have gained your experience.
3. Give tangible evidence of the problems you have solved.
4. Add any special skills, awards or experience that you have.
5. Give some flavour of how you work.

Yvonne lost her job in the communications section of a government department after the arrival of a new boss. Her leaving was disguised as a redundancy. She was looking for another similar job. This is how she wrote her summary paragraph using the formula above:

Journalist and PR specialist with 4 years' experience of handling media enquiries in busy press office at Department of [name]. Skilled at minimizing impact of potentially hostile stories and of promoting good-news stories, expert in handling sensitive issues with ministers and senior civil servants. Managed all press material for the XXX Inquiry [a high-profile Inquiry into a major accident] with aplomb; nominated for an RTS journalism award while at BBC London for investigative work on street gangs; 5 years as reporter on Mirror, 3 years on Guardian, personal blog has average 300 visitors. Unflappable under pressure.

Experience with punch

Apart from being seriously over-length, the biggest single mistake that unaware CV-writers make is to describe responsibilities not achievements. The potential employer does not care about your responsibilities, will have little idea what your impressive-sounding job title means in practice and even less idea of whether you actually made any difference to the bottom line. Anything that leaves a CV-reader with the question 'So what?' is a failure. You were responsible for a budget of £5000, £50,000 or £50 million – so what, what did you do with it? You managed ten staff – so what, did they meet their targets? There is only any point in writing about real achievements – that is times where you went beyond what was asked of you and made a positive difference. Good questions to ask yourself here are:

Question	Examples
What did I improve?	Profit, turnover; innovation rate, quality, relationships with partner organizations;
What decreased?	Sickness absence; wastage; overstocks; unused space; returns; delays; costs; cycle time; customer complaints
What increased?	Staff satisfaction rates on surveys; customer satisfaction; teamwork
What innovations did I introduce?	Policies, strategies, products, more efficient ways of working; better Health and Safety compliance
What crises did I handle well?	Emergencies, bad news, sudden drop in orders, first aid, staff crises

When they look hard at their experience, it surprises many people to realize how much of this they have done, so even where they have had relatively humble or junior jobs, they often have strong stories to tell. So, for instance, a recent graduate had set up an innovative riding scheme for disabled older adults, a

barista working at a coffee chain had acted swiftly and sensibly to stop a nasty fight getting out of hand in her coffee shop in the middle of an urban riot, a young team manager in social services had created a clever new shift system which made maximum use of scarce people-resources, an insurance call-centre worker had achieved outstanding results in selling new policies to existing customers by using a conspicuously warm approach, a volunteer at an emergency shelter had introduced a more effective and respectful way of screening clients for drugs and alcohol.

In writing about achievements, use direct, simple language and avoid feeble words like *did, helped, contributed, had, made, went, got*. Use more powerful words such as *led, managed, produced, initiated, pioneered, launched, devised, directed, solved, organized*. Wherever possible back up your claims with numbers because this gives tangible proof that you made a difference. So instead of writing 'team morale improved' it would be better to say, 'Staff survey demonstrated 17% improvement in team morale'. Instead of 'got excellent A-level results from Year 13 students' say '70% of Year 13 students achieved A* results'. Instead of 'got wastage down to minimum' it has far more power to say, 'Reduced wastage to 1%'. Use numbers: raw numbers, percentages and money wherever you can.

Fail-safe ways of reducing the length of a CV

When you write your first draft CV it will probably be too long – remember that anything over 800 words will look verbose. Don't worry too much at this stage – it is better to start too long, as this will enable you to see your whole career, and then to reduce it to essentials for that pitch for that specific job.

Start by taking out as many of the 'a', 'an' and 'the' words as you can and remove 'I' or 'me'. Précis all those loosely constructed sentences which add little and give the reader more information than they need:

> I worked for ten years as a buyer in Partridge and Pheasant Ltd, the specialist homewares company, where I ended up heading the kitchenware team. While there I travelled extensively on buying trips to China, India and Thailand to search for the quirky and unusual product that our very discerning customers liked. By buying shrewdly and in bulk I was able to achieve great margins for the company. [68 words]

Reworked to less than half the original length, this is how it read:

> 10 years as buyer for Partridge and Pheasant Ltd heading kitchenware team, travelling extensively in the Far East. Achieved 150% margins buying quirky product for our discerning customers. [28 words]

Always choose short words over long ones, so *buy* is better than *purchase*, *start* is better than *commence*, *wrong* is better than *incorrect*. Research shows that people attribute more intelligence to writers of short words than they do to those who persist in using three- or four-syllable words. This is because short words are easier to read and understand. Similarly, avoid the passive tense. The active tense makes the meaning clearer. So write, 'Reduced overruns by 12%' rather than 'Overruns were reduced by 12%'. Ban management jargon, even your favourites, as these phrases tend to alienate by suggesting lazy thinking: for instance *strategic envelope*, *low-hanging fruit*, *thinking out of the box*, *own goal*, *ballpark figure* – and hundreds more.

Now look at how much space you have devoted to your early career. The employer is only really interested in your present or last job, is rather less interested in the one before that and only dimly or not at all in anything that happened more than ten years ago. This means you should put achievements and skills associated with your most recent job on page 1, have maybe one short section on the job before that at the top of page 2 and then summarize the rest as job titles, employers and dates, under the heading *Earlier Career*. If you have had a long earlier career with many job changes then add something like 'details on request'. The exceptions are for jobs in medicine or professions allied to medicine where longer CVs are permitted in order to allow for a full career record, as any gaps could indicate something sinister.

Gut the job specification and look carefully at the person specification. Refer to the notes you have made on the organization and why it needs this job filled at all (see also Chapter 10). Where there is a competency list, that is, a list of the skills attitudes and behaviours that the successful candidate needs, make sure you can produce evidence that your own experience and skills are a close match.

What to leave out

There is no need to include any of these unless specifically asked for: date of birth, driving licence, early schooling, religious affiliation, your current or last salary, reasons for leaving any job, names of referees, marital status, photographs, training courses you have attended (unless some kind of high-profile course which has prestige and where it is difficult to get a place).

Telling the truth

Many careers have involved embarrassments and underachievement, for instance, failing to get a good degree, leaving a job too soon, getting stuck in low-level jobs or in one organization for too long. It can be tempting to decorate the truth – awarding yourself a better degree, renaming a job to sound grander, lengthening the amount of time you spent in a job, inflating salary, taking five years off your age. In a word, don't. The bigger the lie the more negative energy you will need and the harder it becomes to preserve your secret. More often than not employers check – and check everything: awards, licensing PINs, dates, title and salary of previous roles. If it turns out that you have lied, you will be dismissed because the assumption will be that if you can lie about your qualifications and career, your moral compass is generally adrift and no one wants an employee where this is the case.

Jodie was a 22-year-old looking for a first job after a good degree and an MSc course with a top-level university. She took the risk of saying she had already passed her MSc with distinction because she had been told informally that this was the case and also added two weeks to the length of an intern job in an oil company. She did an impressive interview with a big-name consultancy and was offered a well-paid job. Between the offer and her start date, the HR department checked her qualifications and experience, uncovering the way she had been less than truthful. The job offer was swiftly withdrawn.

Personal interests

People often wonder about whether to include this information. The answer is yes, you should include it as it is another way of showing in what ways you are unique. What not to do is to write: *reading, walking, travel, cooking, spending time with my family, films.* Everybody does these things so they do nothing to differentiate you. Say what kinds of books or films you like, what types of home cooking you do, where and how you like to travel – and so on:

Watching Hollywood blockbusters.

Walking in the wilds of Cumbria with close friends.

Gym bunny and Alpine climber.

Experimenting with writing romantic fiction.

Making patchwork quilts for the babies of friends.

Formats

There are many possible formats for a CV and some professions, such as academic posts and medicine, have special requirements which are beyond the space available in this book. Entering *CV Formats* into your search engine will instantly bring up dozens of sites with practical formats and advice. Adding variants such as *CV format/graduate* or *CV format/lawyer* will help refine the search. The point of these searches should be to give you ideas about how a completed CV looks. Never be tempted to adapt a ready-made CV and never let someone else write it for you. The reasons are that the result will be unnatural and impersonal. It will not represent the unique you and to a canny reader it will be obvious what you have done. It is better to submit to the struggle of creating your own. It will become easier each time you do it.

The simplest format is chronological, starting from your present or last job and working backwards. This gives a reader a clear view of your career and interests. Here is a reliable basic framework.

Page 1

Contact details (2 lines)

Your name, address, home email, home phone number, mobile phone number. To get this on 2 lines use the Table menu in Word and then remove the borders

Profile (5 lines – see above page 166)

Achievements and Skills (rest of page 1)

Name of job, employer name, dates including months (1 line)

Responsibilities (1 line)

Bulleted list of what you achieved in the job, closely mirroring what the employer is looking for. Use their wording if you can. About 55 words per skill/achievement

Page 2

Name of previous job, organization, dates as before

Bulleted summary of achievements: about 6 lines

Earlier career

List of jobs, organizations, dates

Qualifications

Name of qualification, name of awarding body, date (start with the most recent and work backwards)

Personal interests

2 lines

Summary

A powerful CV conveys the essence of what you offer an employer, giving a clear view of you and your career, showing how you match what they need. Always tailor the CV for that employer. Two pages of simple, well-presented type is the limit, so it is essential to craft what you write to make a good first impression, eliminating verbiage and jargon, using powerful words and composing a personal profile which will differentiate you as a strong candidate.

Further reading

The CV Book: Your Definitive Guide to Writing the Perfect CV, by James Innes (Pearson, 2012). This is a comprehensive book on creating a CV and has excellent tips on making a CV stand out.

My own book *Great Answers to Tough CV Problems* (Kogan Page, 2011) covers all aspects of writing a CV and includes sample formats.

10 SECRETS OF SUCCESS AT THE INTERVIEW

Possibly there are some people out there who enjoy selection interviews, but if so, I don't meet them often. Far more commonly a candidate will describe anticipating an interview with a knotted stomach, a feeling of doom and of overwhelming anxiety. Myths about interviews abound: *it's all a setup; you should go to an interview even if you don't want the job because it will be good practice for a job you really do want; the questions are bound to be tricky; it's like an exam; interviewers are out to trap you; you can't prepare.* None of these beliefs is supported by the evidence. In this chapter I describe how you can significantly raise your chances of success in the interview by taking several simple steps that will give you the edge over competitors.

Getting your mind in the right place

Most of the myths about job interviews come down to one common theme: the helplessness of the candidate. The truth is that you are not helpless. The interview is a two-way process where you are choosing them as much as they are choosing you and if you are a strong candidate more of the power will lie with you. Interviewers are selling you the job and typically downplay some of its more problematical aspects. It is easy to forget this when you are the candidate. You should get right out of your head any idea that the interview is some kind of *exam, courtroom interrogation* or *inquisition*: all of these are unhelpful metaphors.

It is much better to think of the interview as a social event where you are the guest and they are the hosts. When you are a guest at the invitation of a friend, you will want to show the best possible version of yourself and to take a full part in making the event a success. This is important because research shows clearly that selection panels choose as much on the basis of how the candidate actually *behaves* at the interview as on their professional competence. A job interview is an essentially irrational process, justified later by rationality. This is why it is so vital to see the interview as a place where it is your social skills as much as any intellectual prowess or experience that is being judged, so smiling, having a firm handshake and sitting in a confident, relaxed way can all have as much impact as anything you say.

Solutions for nervousness

Some nervousness is essential as it will give you helpful adrenaline, but too much anxiety is damaging. Many people describe feeling unable to think clearly at a job interview or not being able to remember later what it was that they said, except that they are sure it was something idiotic. There are biological as well as psychological reasons for this. When we are overwhelmingly anxious, a flood of the hormone cortisol shuts down our higher thinking processes because our brains see the interview as a threat and the brain responds in exactly the same way as it would if we were facing a physical threat so our bodies are preparing us to run away by sending oxygen and glucose to muscles. (See also page 4.) But running away is the very thing we cannot do; hence the tension. You should tell yourself that this is normal rather than that you are being 'stupid'. However, you are not the victim of your physiology and there are some simple and effective ways of helping yourself.

7/11 breathing

Try this now. Sit up in your chair, put your shoulders back so that your chest opens out and keep your shoulders down. The aim is to breathe from your diaphragm and in a disciplined way that will calm you down. Put your hands just below your navel with the fingers of each hand splayed and just touching over your belly. Take a deep breath in, focusing on taking it from as low down in your chest as you can. As you do this you should see the space between the two sets of fingers expand. If this space stays firmly the same, you are not breathing from the diaphragm so keep practising until you can do it. Now you are going to practise adding a long out-breath because it is the out-breath that releases anxiety. Make the breathing easy and natural so don't hold your breath between breathing in and breathing out, but do make the out-breath longer. Breathe in, mouth closed, to a steady count of seven and then out at the same rate to a count of 11, gently blowing the air through a slightly open mouth as if you are blowing out a candle. Now be conscious of slowing your breathing right down. As you breathe out, imagine all your anxiety leaving you, mentally saying, 'relaxing . . . relaxing . . .'.

Practise this for at least 10 minutes every day until you can do it easily and automatically. You will find that your body and mind have calmed right down and you will also have taught yourself an association between doing this disciplined breathing and knowing you will be calm. Make sure you do the breathing just before you go into the interview room.

At the same time as practising 7/11 breathing, you can use the power of imagination in the human brain. When we feel anxious we are catastrophizing about all the terrible things that could happen but probably never will; imagination is working vividly though not helpfully. You can play the brain at its own game by consciously visualizing positive outcomes. Set aside some regular time to do this: see yourself in that interview room, being welcomed by pleasant people, smiling back, feeling centred and calm, hearing yourself giving a good account of your skills and leaving feeling pleased with how you have managed the whole event. Programming the brain to expect success counteracts any habits you may have developed of expecting failure.

Preparation that counts

The candidate who does the most thorough preparation is the one who substantially increases their chances of getting the job.

But it has to be the preparation that counts. Your aim is twofold: to double-check whether you want to work in the organization and in that job; to collect information which you can use in the interview itself.

First, you have to research the organization's public face. All employers are vain. They want to hear that you are eager to join them, so you have to find out why this might be the case. Look first at their website; what does it tell you about how they see themselves? Most companies will have a mission statement and a statement of values. These are usually aspirational – how they hope to be rather than how they actually are, so any discrepancy is worth exploring. Enter the company name into your search engine and see what else comes up – for instance newspaper stories, blogs by happy or discontented staff. How are they doing on performance – is it going up or down? What does their staff survey tell you? What issues are they facing in terms of competitors?

The material that is publicly available will give you the surface story so now you have to dig a little deeper. In the job pack there may be a named person, often an HR professional, who can be approached for information. If so then you should call them. The purpose of the call is most definitely not to sell yourself – you are gathering information about the organization and the role and hoping to impress with your diligence and listening skills. Good questions to ask here are:

> What's the reason for the vacancy?
>
> What problems will the successful candidate be expected to solve?
>
> How would you judge whether this person had been successful – say after they had been in the job for six months?
>
> What are the most important skills you're looking for?
>
> Is there any advice you can give me about how to pitch my application?

If you can visit the premises without having to go through security checks, then do so – for instance, if the employer is a shop or a building which is open to the public. What does this tell you about working there? If you pose as a customer, how are you treated?

After this, a little light espionage can come in handy. Who do you or might you know in this organization? Here you can ask all the questions above, but you should also ask about the culture of the organization: 'What is it like to work in it? What do people get rewarded or punished for? Would you recommend that a friend joined it? What do you know about the person who would be my boss if I got the job?' Bear in mind that the answers may well be gossip and therefore unreliable, but what is gossiped about is also telling, so this is not a reason to avoid hearing it.

Normally when you are shortlisted you will be told who is on the interview panel. Google all of them, checking their LinkedIn profiles and Twitter feeds so that you get some idea of what interests and preoccupies them. Most of these sources will have photographs; memorize the faces so that you can confidently address them by name during the interview.

Preparation that has low value but that can take up enormous amounts of time, such as reading business plans, strategy papers, legislation, or background detail about the history of the organization, will only pay off if you are competing for a Board-level post and you should see it as an optional addition to all the other research I mention above.

If what you uncover during this process tells you plainly that the job is a poor fit for your skills, or that you would hate working for the boss or the organization, then withdraw at this point. It is never worth going to an interview for a job you don't want; it would be immediately apparent to the panel, you would not get the job and you would not feel good about yourself as a result.

There is no mystery about the questions

The myth persists that interviewers ask cranky, inexplicably torturing questions that no one can see coming. The truth is much more positive. Interviewers for the most part ask 90% predictable questions and you can prepare for all of them in advance. The actual wording of the questions is, of course, not predictable, but the question areas are. There are only eight that are ever probed at a job interview and for each of them there is an underlying, unstated interviewer anxiety. In preparing your answers you should address the underlying anxiety as well as the question that is actually asked.

Question as asked	Real question
What are you currently doing?/Tell us a bit about yourself/Talk us through your CV	*Are you doing anything that is at all relevant to what we want? Are you going to bore us with a description of every tedious aspect of your current or last role?*
Why do you want this job?	*Is this person a time-waster? Are your reasons for wanting the job the ones that we want to hear? If we offered you the job, would you accept?*
What skills do you think this job will need?	*How realistic is your grasp of what the job needs?*
How good a match are your skills to what this job needs? (NB that this normally forms the bulk of the interview on the basis of a competency framework sent to you in advance)	*Do you have any proper track record of doing what we need or is it all bluff and blarney? What evidence can you give us?*
What problems do you anticipate this job holder will meet?	*How much proper research have you done into the job? Are you a tactless critic who will tell us the unwelcome news that we've made mistakes?*
What are your strengths and weaknesses? Sometimes asked as, What are you most proud of/sorry about in the last year?	*Do you really know for certain how you strike others? Or are you in a little bubble of unwarranted self-esteem?*

How good a match are your personal circumstances to what this job needs?	*Can't ask you about sexual orientation or marital status but is there anything about your domestic life, health etc. that would prevent you doing this job properly?*
What questions do you have for us?	*Are your questions about yourself for instance salary and benefits – or, what we want to hear – about us?*

Answering the why you want the job question in four easy steps

This could be the most important single question in the interview and is normally asked as the first or second question. It tests your motivation (one of the few factors that a traditional interview can test properly), your research and your ability to subtly flatter the panel. Many candidates throw away their chances at this stage because their answer is all about me, me and more of me: why it suits their career path, why the salary is attractive, why they are/were bored with their current/last role or don't/didn't get on with their boss. The employer is not interested in your career problems, only in how you could solve their problems and if you seem disloyal to your current employer they will assume that you are a disloyal person generally. Here is how to answer using four easily remembered steps:

1. You are attracted to the organization because [you list the attractive features you have uncovered in your research: its mission and purpose, its values, its reputation for x and y, the kind of culture it has, which you describe].
2. There is a good fit with your personal values [you list them].
3. You can see that the job needs the skills of a and b, because you have done as much thorough research as

you can as an outsider into the problems the job holder will be solving and you believe you have those skills [you list them].

4. Finally, you loved your last job but this would be a challenging and attractive next step.

Giving SPAR evidence-based answers to all the other questions

Standards of interviewing are generally not high. Interviewers rarely get trained and often overrate their own ability to ask brief, clear, insightful questions. They may be ignorant of the law on equality. They may be pompous, they may ask vague, double, triple or quadruple questions. They may also be capable of asking absurd hypothetical questions, the most absurd of which I ever heard was, 'If the Thames Barrier gave way on the same day that there was a terrorist attack on London, how would you deal with your staff?'[3] Even when guided to ask competency-based questions, these can be garlanded with so many dependent clauses plus unnecessary adverbs and adjectives that the poor candidate is left floundering.

Preparing by studying the competency list is vital as a way of anticipating what the question means, but if in doubt, ask politely for more clarification.

The naive interviewee answers questions with assertions and in the second person (using the words *you* or *one*). The naive interviewer makes it worse by asking a poorly focused question such as, 'What is your approach to leading a team?' The naive interviewee then replies with an answer that could have come straight out of a management textbook. 'Well, you have to tread

3 This is an absurd and unfair question because any large organization will have emergency planning systems in place and most candidates, especially if external, are unlikely to know what they are.

a careful line between consulting people too much and not consulting them at all. One must remember at all times to . . . bla bla bla'. This tells the interviewer nothing about this person's actual practice, only that they have read the textbooks. This candidate will be told later that the reason they did not get the job was that they did not answer the questions fully. This may be unfair, but that is the impression he or she will have given.

Storytelling and why it works

You have 2–3 minutes, no more, to answer any question. The secret here is to make sure that every answer contains a tightly packed story about how you tackled a specific problem relating to whichever competency is being probed. Storytelling works because the human brain loves narrative, so by telling a story you are serving several powerful purposes at once: keeping the panel entertained and awake (they probably have a long and tiring day), giving them evidence of your social skills through your performance as a storyteller and giving them actual evidence of your track record and how you work. SPAR is a helpful way of remembering the framework for any successful story

S	Situation (20 seconds)	The general background: how things appeared to be going along normally
P	Problem (40 seconds)	The sudden disruption to the normal: how it was a crisis; what was at stake for the organization; the barriers that had to be overcome by you and others; some brief references to the people involved and your own feelings at the time
A	Action (1 minute 30 seconds)	What you actually did: how you overcame the barriers step by step, how you persuaded people, what their responses were, what your own feelings were as the process went on
R	Results (20 seconds)	The tangible and successful impact that your actions had, remembering to quote numbers, percentages, money, whenever you can

I strongly recommend that you learn and apply this technique. I believe it is the reason that, when skilfully applied, around 75% of my coaching clients get the jobs they have competed for.

Some additional hints

Say *I* not *we*. The panel wants to know what *you*, and not what some vague collective presence, did. If you keep using *we*, a panel can get irritated and will potentially waste interview time, which could be spent on other questions, asking what your personal contribution actually was. At the same time, much organizational effort is collective, so it is fine to intersperse *I* with the occasional *we*. 'I developed the outline plan for the project [you describe this] and then I had to bring my team on board [you say how]. We then had regular project meetings which I chaired, where we checked on how far we were meeting our milestones. I also made sure that everyone had an individual set of targets.'

Bring your answers alive with dialogue and storyteller's techniques. If you have read or told stories to children, these stories will always have dialogue which can be said with emphasis and funny voices. You don't have to use funny voices in a job interview but you can introduce a little drama by hinting at characterization and by occasionally sprinkling, 'So I said', and 'He said' or by using louder or softer volume, faster or slower pace.

Answering questions about redundancy

When you have actually left your last job because of redundancy you can expect a question asking why. Redundancy is no longer a strange, puzzling and unusual event, so these questions are easier to answer than used to be the case. The secret is to keep the reply brief, to avoid any whiff of anger and of appearing to blame your previous employer, putting the emphasis on the financial pressures facing the previous organization:

The government told us we had to make 25% cuts and head-count was the obvious place. Unfortunately my department was one of those chosen for the axe.

The company had been trading in adverse circumstances for about a year – we issued a profit warning last summer and went into liquidation two months ago.

The new CEO wanted to recruit a new team and radically reorganize so my job disappeared along with those of three of my colleagues.

Our market for this product went into steep decline and the executive team asked for voluntary redundancies. I leapt at the chance because I felt it was time I made a move.

When asked what you have been doing during a period of unemployment, the best answer is to talk enthusiastically about using the time to rethink your career, do volunteer work and catch up with any personal development involving training.

> Bryn was one of several staff made redundant by a struggling university. After the initial shock he followed much of the advice in this book, including making sure he did some volunteering. In answering this question when competing for a different type of job with another university he said, 'This has been one of the most important periods of my life. I've stood back, taken stock of my skills, and used the time very fruitfully. I've decided I want a mainstream academic job and don't want to continue along the managerial route. While I've been out of work I've been a volunteer for a local adult literacy project where it was mandatory to do some exceptionally rigorous training. This has made me reconsider everything I thought I knew about teaching and I'll definitely be a better HE teacher as a result'.

One of the most important pieces of preparation you can do for the interview is to assemble a total of around 15 anecdotes which roughly cover each competency area and to practise telling them in a compelling way. This is practice, by the way, and not rehearsal. Never *rehearse* as in learning a script. You will get stuck trying to remember your script – or thrown because the interviewer does not ask the question in exactly the way you anticipated.

Two days before the interview, ask the most ruthless member of your support group (page 67) to run through a practice interview with you. Listen carefully to their feedback and ask them to let you re-try any of your weaker attempts.

Looking the part

Part of your research should be into the dress code in your target organization. Whatever the answer, bump it up one notch in formality for the interview. Even in places where people dress casually, they may do a smarter variant for an interview. If in doubt, ask. It is usually safer to be more rather than less formal. Go for structured clothing in whichever plain darkish colours are right for your skin and hair and please note that there are comparatively few people who look good in black. If you have very light skin, ashy hair and pale blue eyes and then dress in black from top to toe with a stark white shirt you run the risk of looking either like an undertaker or a member of the waiting team. There should be a minimum of visible flesh and nothing that dangles, flaps, strains or gapes. Everything you wear should be in immaculate condition: no bobbles, shiny wear-marks, food stains, holes, fraying cuffs or unpolished shoes. If your appearance suggests dishevelment the panel may assume the same is true of your working style.

It can be hard to control body language that leaks clues about any remaining nervousness you may have, but you should try. Before the interview, practise keeping both feet firmly planted on the floor, sitting with your bottom tucked into the back of a chair, shoulders down, hands resting lightly on your lap, face looking straight ahead. Your aim is relaxed authority. Practise keeping your voice up, speaking a little more slowly than normal. Practise answering questions without any of those give-away gestures that suggest uncertainty, for instance twirling legs around the chair, touching your face, tweaking or playing with spectacles, plucking invisible fluff from sleeves.

Eye contact matters. When answering a question from one panel member, sweep the others with constant eye contact by moving your head to include them in the answer. Remember to smile as you answer, especially if you know you have the habit of frowning while you give yourself time to think. A frown can look like a scowl; not an attractive proposition.

Summary

You increase your chances of success at a job interview by thorough preparation into the organization, the job and the people on the panel. Interview questions are predictable and you can prepare for them by assembling convincing stories which follow the SPAR framework. Look the part by dressing impeccably and keeping body language under control.

Further reading

What Color is Your Parachute? (page 125) has an excellent section on being interviewed.

My own book *Job Interview Success: Be Your Own Coach* (McGraw-Hill Professional, 2011) covers every aspect of job interviews including preparing for assessment centres and negotiating salary.

11 THE ALTERNATIVE LIFE

In this chapter I look at alternatives to conventional employment and the kinds of issues you need to consider before deciding whether this is the right path for you.

In my thirties I remember being in awe of BBC colleagues who cheerfully left what was then very secure employment to go freelance. It seemed like an act of unutterable daring: didn't they worry about how they would get work? How come they seemed so calm and so certain it was the right decision? At the time I had two small children, a frighteningly large mortgage, a husband whose health problems were beginning to become chronic and a great deal of career frustration, feeling stuck in a job (TV producer) that had become dull and predictable. It simply never occurred to me that going freelance could be the solution to my dilemmas.

A decade later, I had left the BBC to go into publishing and had then returned in a managerial role, running a learning and development department. It slowly became obvious to me that this role was destined for redundancy at some point in the not too distant future and, simultaneously, that my interest in executive coaching was not going to go away. The wish to leave became a compulsion. The end of parenting was in sight, the mortgage had diminished and I realized I could probably earn more as a freelance to pay for any care needed by my husband. I left without any agonizing, in much the same carefree way that I had observed in colleagues all those years earlier.

I was proved right that my former job would disappear and leaving before this became a reality suited me well. It may be different for you, but the point is that depending on your circumstances, temperament and life-stage, the alternative life might be a good choice.

Typical reasons for going freelance

There can be many different reasons for deciding to follow the freelance route.

Temperament. Some people are profoundly uneasy with corporate life. The career anchor Autonomy (page 115) describes them well. They view meetings as a baffling waste of time where nothing ever gets decided; they don't see much point in a boss – why have someone who just gets in the way? They resent attempts to impose targets. The sociable aspect of corporate life has little appeal because it is bought at the price of conforming; it is better to be able to come and go at will. If this describes you then redundancy may be welcome. You can be your own boss and live with the consequences.

My newspaper was in the grip of financial problems: a combination of a huge drop in advertising revenue and the rise of online services. Initially I felt resentful about the redundancy but I soon came to see that it was liberating. I was well connected and landed a few columns as well as being offered the chance to edit an online magazine. I realized I need never go into that office again, sit at Conference listening to idiots prattle on, pretending to agree with things I didn't agree with. I can do what I really love which is the journalism. In theory I don't earn as much but in practice I have more money in my pocket as so many ordinary expenses are tax-deductable.

Passionately held interest that must be pursued. It is not uncommon to get promoted out of your technical specialism and into a managerial role. Sometimes it is the only way to earn more money and to get promotion, but for some people it never feels quite right even though they may do the actual work well. Where the specialism is one that can be pursued as self-employment, the choice to follow that path can become irresistible.

Don't need the money, do need the sense of purpose is a variant on this. As part of the all-round reappraisal that redundancy can create, there are people who decide to make a whole-life switch

and this will often involve working for themselves. Their financial circumstances may vary from not at all well off to seriously wealthy; it doesn't seem to matter, as what motivates them is the sense of keying in to their true life purpose. Whether they make any money in their new lives they see as less important than being happy and fulfilled.

Jean-Claude had done well in the finance sector but had become increasingly uncomfortable with his way of life and the values he saw around him. A small blip in what had otherwise been a smooth route to business success and a shrinkage in his firm, jolted him into rethinking why he was still single at 42 and was spending so many weekends alone. He decided to opt for voluntary redundancy. He had had a long fascination with viticulture and plunged all of his savings into a struggling vineyard in France, knowing that it could be five years, if then, before it broke even. His comment: 'I needed to ground myself in a real place, put down roots. No regrets. I am literally connected with the earth and doing something I love.'

At the other end of the wealth spectrum, I have worked with clients who start with very little money and opt for even less.

Al was a schoolteacher and had always been a seriously committed Christian. When his school decided that it had one Deputy Head too many, Al put his hand up to leave. He had already retrained as an Anglican priest. As a widower with grown children he felt that he could live perfectly well on his small pension. He discovered a spiritually rewarding niche in conducting funerals for families who were not churchgoers but wanted a religious ceremony, supplementing this work with a little income from marking exam papers.

Personal circumstances. When redundancy coincides with a major change in personal circumstances, freelance work can seem attractive.

> My partner had been the stay-at-home parent while I built my career. Redundancy changed everything. We decided that she could resume her career while I became the main carer for our children and that I could probably earn at least something by working as a web designer from home, a task I relished as of all the aspects of my previous job, this was the one I had enjoyed most and I was certain I could make a go of it.

Frustration and boredom. I have worked with many senior people who have a growing feeling of disenchantment with corporate life. They have been professional managers for most of their careers but now it has lost its charm. Typically these people are in their late fifties or early sixties, they have already been at the top of their particular pyramids, they are secure financially, with pensions and savings. They may have competed half-heartedly for other senior jobs but the process of competing has told them that they no longer want the stress and long hours of a very senior role and it has been a relief, even though sometimes a temporary blow to their pride, not to be offered the job. They feel too young to retire, so self-employment can look like a viable option.

Prejudices. It is hard to prove whether a potential employer is prejudiced against you – for instance, because of your age, appearance, ethnic origins, sexual orientation or the circumstances of your redundancy. It is always possible that such prejudice is at work and the decision justified on some other grounds. However, an employer who would hesitate to take you on as a full-time member of staff may be more than happy to hire you as a freelance. Two friends from my former field, TV,

definitely a young person's game, are working successfully as jobbing studio directors, work they still enjoy after 35 years at it, despite being twice the age of most of the people in the companies who employ them.

Exhausted other options. When the work you want to do is in short supply and the process of fighting for one of the few jobs that is available has led nowhere, setting up your own business can make sense.

De'ron loved food and cooking. He completed his catering training and after a few years of experience in London hotel kitchens he had a row with his boss, was made redundant and tried without success to find another job that paid more than the low salary he had been earning, as he now had a wife and baby to provide for. Minimum-wage work was plentiful but would not pay the bills. After a discouraging few months of casual work, De'ron decided to start his own business, catering for London's large Afro-Caribbean community, aiming at clients hosting large parties and who wanted the traditional Caribbean food which was familiar to De'ron from his childhood.

The bridge. Self-employment can seem like an attractive option as a bridge between one job and another. This tactic has a lot going for it. It keeps you busy and will probably stretch your skills and give you confidence. When a potential new employer asks what you have been doing since your last job you will be able to talk a good story. However, you do need to be careful with this one. The employer may also want to know why, if the self-employed life is so successful, you want to give it up so you need to have a plausible reply ready, for instance that it is successful financially but you miss working in a team. My own view is that there is a more serious danger lurking. If you secretly yearn for a full-time conventional role then you should be putting a lot of energy into finding it. If you want to build a freelance business then that, too, should be taking all your energy. You can end up splitting your time and doing neither successfully.

However I have observed several clients navigate this difficulty skilfully. They have assumed that they will be spending the rest of their careers as freelancers and have worked diligently at their businesses. At the same time, they are aware that they dislike the instability of freelance work and have had a little script ready if people have asked them whether they would be attracted by a conventional job.

> *I would say, I'm really enjoying what I do and I like the freedom, but if the right job came up, and it would have to be the right job, I would certainly consider it.*
>
> *I'm committed to building my business for the foreseeable future, and at the moment I'm planning to give it a good three years, but if a good job in [Y sector] running [A or B thing] were to appear with an attractive salary then I might embark on a flirtation . . .*

Statements like these make it clear there is no desperation but that for the right job you might be interested.

How much would you like self-employment?

When self-employment is one of the options you are considering, this questionnaire gives you a chance to consider your initial responses to the whole idea. Essentially it's about the balance between how much you would like the autonomy that self-employment brings and how much you would fear the lack of stability and predictability that is also part of life for most self-employed people.

Tick the column that represents how much you would like any of these features of the self-employed life.

Key: 3 = an important factor for you, 2 = a moderately important factor, 1 = not important.

Yes, I'd enjoy the possibility of this	3	2	1
Only doing the work I want to do			
Managing my own working day			
Possibly working from home			
Freedom from organizational politics			
Enjoying the risk factor			
Getting a direct relationship between activity and income			
Setting my own targets			
Being able to blend work and private life			
Working with a range of organizations and people			
Being potentially able to increase my income from its present level			
Being able to use all my abilities			
Choosing exactly how hard I want to work			
Total for potential enjoyment factors			

Now do the same for this list – the factors that may be discouragers and a disincentive to self-employment.

Key: 3 = a serious disincentive; 2 = a mild disincentive, 1 = not a disincentive.

Yes, I could find this a discourager/disincentive	3	2	1
Missing the 9-5 discipline			
Not having the legitimate opportunity to get away from domestic concerns during the day (if working from home)			

continued

Yes, I could find this a discourager/disincentive	3	2	1
Getting easily distracted; lacking self-discipline			
Missing low-key chores such as meetings which offer pleasant excuses to avoid more demanding work			
Having to sell myself and fearing rejection			
Not having the predictability of a regular salary			
Bored and irritated by admin chores			
Feeling lonely on my own			
Missing the security of knowing one organization in depth			
Not having a boss who can coach and support me – having to do this for myself			
Knowing that work flow can sometimes be unpredictable – 'feast or famine' and fearing having little control over it			
Over-working out of fear that the next job will be the last			
Total for potential disincentives/dissuaders			

There are 12 items in each list.

How do your totals compare? Are there some items in each list that you rate ***super-important***? If so, give them each an extra 2 points.

What is the balance between the two lists? How does this leave you feeling now?

In a nutshell, self-employment gives you control over your career and life but it comes at the price of risk and unpredictability.

Running a business is a serious business

The biggest single mistake I see people make in setting up their own businesses is failing to understand that it is not just about working away at the trade, profession or skill that you love. You are running a small business and like any other business it is essential to look squarely at all of these factors:

Competitors: if they are successful, what portion of the market would be left for you? What can you learn from how they are doing?

Fees and prices: what's the going rate in your area for your type of work or product?

What's your market niche? What defines your typical customer? What problems can you solve for them?

What is your competitive advantage, sometimes described as your Unique Selling Proposition (USP), the skills and knowledge that give you an edge over competitors and that it would be hard for them to reproduce?

What would be left over from any earnings after you have paid for your costs? Would this justify the effort it would take to earn the money?

Do you want to grow this company so that it has capital value and ultimately is saleable?

How do you feel about selling your services? Does your fear of rejection get in the way? Are you confident about selling with integrity?

Marketing: how will you promote your service or product?

Business development

Most small businesses need a period of business development before they are profitable, that is, research, planning, doing early projects and seeing how they land, getting feedback and building contacts – and this typically takes a year to 18 months. The process is an exact mirror of the approach in earlier chapters where you map your network, and develop and build a brand. As with looking for a conventional job, it is virtually always better to aim narrowly than broadly. While you are building the business you need to know that you can keep going financially, either by dipping into your savings or by asking a partner to subsidize you, remembering that you will also have costs to cover: computers, National Insurance, indemnity insurance, training, setting up a website, phones, at least some professional advice from designers, accountants and lawyers, buying drinks or lunches for useful contacts, travel. It helps to develop a simple business plan, writing a few paragraphs on your USP and your target market and then forecasting monthly income against expenses. For your first year you should also estimate overall turnover, making three forecasts: optimistic, pessimistic and realistic.

Remember, too, that there may be no one but you to stand in the post office queue, set up meetings and run some kind of simple accounting system. Even with a business which is cash in hand, this needs to be logged and expenses monitored, as Her Majesty's Revenue and Customs (HMRC) is merciless.

> Harley was made redundant from a nationally known chain of hairdressing salons when the recession began to bite. Well trained, he believed he could go it alone, renting a chair in a micro-salon run by a friend. 'I got in a muddle', he says, 'having decided I would only work with cash, didn't want the hassle of credit cards, but I began to lose track of what I was taking, using it as petty cash for personal expenses and wasn't thinking clearly about what my outgoings were. Doing my tax return was a nightmare. I realized I needed to set up a proper system for the future.'

The danger of seeing self-employment as a hobby or an escape

Some people leave managerial jobs with a reasonable pay-off and feel that it would be pleasant to do what they often describe

as 'a little consultancy work'. At first it seems to go well – for instance, their former employer will offer them a project or two. Two years later the consultancy work has dried up, the would-be consultant is mildly peeved but has become immersed in leisure or voluntary activities. The reason this has happened is that he or she has seen consultancy as a hobby, something to be picked up and put down at will. The consultant may also be in a double bind – quickly seen as part of the past and out of touch by potential clients in his or her former company and yet still too associated with it to attract other clients.

The commercial world is ruthless. To run a consultancy, or indeed any small business, you have to be serious, focused and highly motivated, updating your skills and knowledge, constantly nudging your market. They soon forget you if you do none of this.

There are other popular fantasies associated with self-employment, usually involving escaping from the city to live in rural peace: for instance, running a B&B or a country pub, having a boutique in a small town, breeding puppies, keeping a livery stable. All of these forms of self-employment involve investing serious money and are time-consuming; the only reason for doing them is that you really truly love the whole idea, have investigated it thoroughly, have relevant experience and a talent for the tasks. One former client of mine who did actually leave his stressful chief executive role to run a B&B told me later that he had never worked so hard in his life.

Whatever the business, you cannot assume that what seems to be a successful formula today will be a successful formula next year; you have to watch the trends closely and have a sales pipeline. The work is relentless and I notice how many newly self-employed people do exactly as I did at the start-up phase which was to work around the clock and the week. Assuming you have talent and have done your homework on your market, you will succeed – but it takes determination and energy.

Interim work

Working as an interim manager can be attractive as a halfway house between conventional employment and a freelance life. Interims work on assignments which can be anything from a few weeks to six months or more in length, paid on a lucrative day rate. Most interims aim to be in paid work for about 140 days a year. The same essential rules apply as to any other kind of freelance activity; interim work is a career in itself, not a convenient stop gap while you look around for something permanent. Unlike other forms of consultancy, you do more than just analyse and advise – you get right in there and run it.

Who needs an interim manager?

Interim assignments are triggered by an immediate short-term need, often a crisis. Examples would be an organization where fraud has been uncovered; a senior manager has left suddenly because of bad publicity; someone in a key post has a serious health problem and will be off sick for several months; an industry regulator has stepped in and demanded change. These circumstances all point to the special qualities that an interim needs: an extremely steady temperament, the ability to analyse quickly and then to implement whatever needs to be done without caring too much whether people like you. Often the work is about clearing up a mess and getting the organization ready for the permanent successor. You know you will just be doing a few months and then moving on. Essentially you will always be an outsider so it is not a career for someone who needs to feel part of the work family or who likes to see long-term results.

Interim work can take you anywhere so you have to be prepared to live out of a suitcase for long periods and to accept that you may only see your family at weekends. Like any other kind of freelance activity, most work is found through personal networks and word-of-mouth recommendation (though there are also agencies which specialize in interim assignments) and while

you are working on one assignment you need to be setting up the next, but even so there can be periods where the diary goes quiet. Most interims accept that this is all part of the life.

Potential employers like to see a managerial career that has been specialist rather than generalist; they look for track record in particular industries and roles because they expect you to be able to jump straight into the work with minimal need for briefing and learning the job. If you compete for this type of role you should make sure that this is what your CV conveys. It makes a good impression if it is clear that you are committed to the interim life by having your own limited company as this suggests permanence and seriousness. The selection process tends to be more informal than for long-term jobs but even so, the same principles about how to behave in a job interview (Chapter 10) apply as you will usually have at least one competitor.

Buying a franchise

Buying a franchise is an option for people who like the idea of self-employment but at the same time would like to minimize risk. The size of the investment will vary according to the nature of the franchise. When you buy a franchise you pay for an established product or service and are guaranteed that you will have no competitors within the same franchise in an agreed geographical area. You are paying for the marketing, publicity, product and – you hope – quality. Many well-known businesses, for instance, Boots Opticians and McDonald's restaurants are franchises. When you go into any McDonald's restaurant you know that the product, quality and service will be identical to what you would find in any other branch.

The franchise company chooses its franchisees carefully, supplies the product, trains you and does all the marketing. In most franchises, the franchisee pays a royalty on sales. The attractions are that you are buying into a recognized brand, it is not complicated to research the business opportunity and to assess how well other franchisees are doing. Banks like franchises because they are known quantities, so borrowing can be relatively easy.

A successful franchisee loves the product or service and has an entrepreneurial mindset, understanding that you still have to attract customers with outstanding service, despite whatever help the franchisor gives you. You have to have a good business brain, know how to manage staff and be willing to submit to the discipline of running the service according to someone else's rules. Like any other form of self-employment it is hard work and the returns can vary from outstanding to disappointing. This is why it is essential to investigate carefully before buying. Go to franchise exhibitions, talk to people already holding a franchise, and in fact do all the research you would do with any other business proposition: competitors, potential customers, likely turnover, likely profit margin. Make a business plan and be prepared to walk away if investigation shows that the prospects of success are poor or that the fit with your skills and needs is not good.

A portfolio career?

The Irish management philosopher Charles Handy coined the phrase *portfolio career* in his remarkably prescient book *The Age of Unreason*, first published in 1989 (Century Hutchinson). He correctly forecast the time when long-term full-time employment would be replaced by a patchwork of short-term contracts, part-time jobs and self-employment. The word *portfolio* conveys the essence of the idea: that you carry your skills with you, they are portable, you sell them in whichever market needs what you offer under a variety of terms and conditions including giving your work away to worthy causes. Charles Handy has also commented that in preparing his own children to leave education he advised them to think in terms of customers, not bosses; wise advice for anyone looking for work in today's economy.

Usually there is one core profession or activity which can be adapted to a variety of purposes. Here are some examples:

Simon has always been adept at writing and editing. His current portfolio includes copy-editing where he works on demand for two publishers, a little graphic design for a friend who runs a website design company, ghost writing for authors who have ideas but no writing talent, rewriting PhD theses for non-native English speakers, caring for his 4-year-old son two days a week and learning sign language with the idea that he could become a professional interpreter.

Becky has a call-off contract with several small firms in East Anglia to provide HR services and also works two days a week as an HR adviser to a law firm in Norwich. She has expertise in family history and runs a popular course at a local community college on how to trace your ancestors.

Eric was an IT specialist, made redundant after a 25-year career with a construction company. He offers a project management service for other IT managers and this takes up about 60 days a year of reasonably well-paid work which he is assiduous in promoting. He is an expert birdwatcher, spends a lot of his now much freer time in the Orkneys or Norfolk, blogs about birds and has more than 5000 followers on Twitter. He loves his work as a non-executive director of a small nature conservancy charity, for which he receives an honorarium but says, 'Frankly, I would do it for nothing, it's so worthwhile. I do around 40 days a year for them and actually I'm acting as a very cheap IT Director!'

Like any other kind of self-employment, portfolio careers benefit from close management, good planning, studying your market and anticipating what it needs. Without this kind of attention 'portfolio' can just come to mean a haphazard and unsatisfying hotchpotch of random activity where you are blown hither and thither by the whims of the market rather than feeling in control – the intrinsic purpose and core benefit of self-employment.

The good life

The word *retirement* chills me because it suggests retiring from life. But sometimes the idea of living *The Good Life*, as satirized in the gentle British comedy of the 1970s, taps a nerve of need in many people. In the TV series, Tom and Barbara Good try to live a self-sufficient life with chickens, a pig and allotments in their Surbiton semi, while their astonished but kindly neighbours Jerry and Margot Leadbetter look on. The comedy came from how extremely difficult it was to be what would now be termed *green*, for instance when the Goods try haplessly to dye their own wool with nettles or turn manure from their animals into methane gas for their car. At the same time, the series mocked middle-class pretentiousness, personified in Margot's rampant snobbery – she does not want chickens skittering about in her garden – and Jerry's self-serving ambition, working in a company that supplies products that no one really needs. Forty years on, the Goods' preoccupations seem less unusual as it becomes clearer that we all need to walk more lightly on the planet.

I am writing this chapter in the Hérault region of France, sitting at a table overlooking the river in the home of some long-standing English friends. They bought this house 25 years ago, when it was in a sadly dilapidated state, repairing and improving it when funds permitted, but always retaining its essence as a typical Cevenole house. They are the least materialistic people I know, living a contented self-sufficient life, growing and cooking most of what they eat, well settled into their village because they speak excellent French. Their car is 20 years old – not at all unusual in an area where many people have little money. As far as I can see they spend nothing on buying fripperies such as new clothing or

'designer' objects of any kind. The log fire warms the big kitchen in the evenings, burning driftwood copiously swept down the river from the heavily forested mountain above, the wine flows freely, the food is delicious, their home a relaxing haven of common sense and good cheer for their many visitors. It is not that they have been 'lucky', though perhaps they would say that they have. They have made their own luck, deciding to let their careers gently peter out as they got older and to live in a way that puts family, relationships and community at the heart of everything they do. If their set-up sounds romantic, a moment's contemplation would show you that it is nothing of the sort. An ancient house is always crumbling somewhere, the many hectares of land will constantly have something that needs seeding, planting, watering, fertilizing, hoeing, pruning, harvesting. Personally I would not last a week if I were responsible for it, but it is just right for my friends. It mirrors their fiercely held values about what matters.

Some people describe my friends as having 'retired', though there is no way that retirement adequately captures the ceaseless activity of their lives. People of retirement age are now often continuing to work, as indeed I am, though more frequently in the kinds of portfolio career I have described earlier in this chapter. They will typically describe themselves as busier than ever. They may be offering substitute parenting for their grandchildren, taking up new interests that they have never had time to pursue before, having more frequent holidays, offering services on a volunteer basis, pursuing a degree through the Open University as well as continuing with part-time or freelance paid work.

Further reading

There are many books on self-employment and a number of free downloadable guides. One of the most comprehensive books is *Self Employment for Dummies* by Colin Barrow (3rd edition, Wiley, 2011). It covers the basics of starting up as well as topics such as employing staff and business growth.

Summary: Career Management in the 21st century

In the end it comes down to answering the questions, *What's my life purpose? What really matters to me? What brings me joy and satisfaction? What legacy do I want to leave?* In the business world, companies are often trapped by their own previous triumphs, failing to see young upstart competitors creeping up on them. It is the same for individuals. You can never assume that your former successes will be enough to guarantee that you will get or keep a job because the emphasis is on what is needed in the here and now. I find that most of my clients get to understand this. From viewing redundancy as a disaster they come to see it as waking them up to a new world of possibilities and living a better life. I will give the last word to Frances, one of the most initially frightened and upset clients I have ever worked with:

> No one could have been more scared than I was at facing redundancy. I'd been in the same place for 22 years, I'd never had to write a CV, I believed my skills were non-transferable even though I have an accountancy qualification, and I thought that I would be living on miserable benefits for ever. What I found was release – it forced me to rethink everything, to value my skills, to see that they had cash value and to relaunch myself. I now work 5 minutes from home so immediately saved the £4000 I'd been spending on a season ticket. I'm the part-time Finance Director for a local arts organization and I also freelance for innumerable small businesses. Essentially these are lovely creative people like photographers and designers who are not good at, or interested in, doing their accounts and tax returns. I even earn more than I did before. Would I ever go back to how things were before? NEVER!

Index

ACAS 32
acceptance 13
achievements 168–9
adjustment 14–15
advisers 50–2
age-barriers 19–20
agencies 58–61
alternatives
  to employment 193–209
  to redundancy 30–1
anger 12, 13–14, 38–9
anxiety 7–8
aptitudes 119–21, 171
autonomy 8–9
avoidance action 75–6, 81–2, 132–3

befrienders 50–1
blogging 155
body language 188–9
breaking the news 25–30
budgeting 89–102
business cards 148
business ventures 200–2

career choices 112–18, 206–8
  see also job choices; life choices
career coaching 55–8
career history 168–9, 170–2
causes of redundancy 71–5
certainty 7–8
change curve/cycle 12–13
charity shops 96
'closure' 20
clothing purchases 96–7
coaching 55–8
colleagues 9–10, 37–8, 40–2
competencies 114, 171, 184, 188
contract of employment 32
control, personal 18–19
coping strategies 11–21
counsellors 51
courses 159
credit cards 93–4
CVs 163–74

denial 12
depression 52
diary keeping 17
discrimination 19–20, 33, 79
dress code 188

early retirement 208–9
early warning 75, 80–1
eating out 100
economic factors 71–5, 132–3
'elevator speech' 123–4

emotional response 3–5, 11–14, 15, 38–40
employee selection
  recruitment 58–64, 143–4, 177–89
  redundancies 77, 78–9
employers
  choices for redundancies 78–80
  giving notice 25–32
  offer 29–30, 31, 65
  recruitment methods 58–64, 143–4
  researching 180–1
  selecting 132, 136–7
employment agencies 58–61
employment tribunals 33–4
entertainments 100
enthusiasms 111–12
excuses 19–20
exercise 100–1
exit script 40–3, 186–7
expenditure 89–102
experience 168–9, 170–1

Facebook 153
fairness 10–11
family 49–50, 90–1
finance, personal 87–103
financial package 31, 93
finding work 19, 143–56
food purchases 97–9
franchises 205–6
freelance work 193–203
friends 49–50

gadgets 94–5
gifts 101–2

head-hunters 61–4
healthcare 53
healthy living 158–9
help 49–68
  see also coping strategies; legal advice
human needs 5–11

ideal job 120–1, 122
individual choices 75–8
informing employees 25–30
interests, personal 111–12, 172
interim work 204–5
internet 152–5
interviews
  recruitment 177–89
  research 148–50

job boards 155
job choices 120–3, 129–37
  see also career choices
job competition 131–2
job interviews 177–89
job perceptions 130–1
job search 143–56
job status 5–7
journal keeping 17

keeping fit 100–1

language of response 16–18
leaving 36–7
leaving parties 43–4
legal action 33–5
legal advice 32, 35, 65
leisure 100
letter writing 150–2
life choices 108–10, 208–9
LinkedIn 153–4
listeners 50–1
locus of control 18–19

meetings, redundancy 27–32
money issues 87–103

negotiation 30–1
networking 145–8
notice of redundancy 25–30
notice period 31, 32, 35–6

older workers 19–20
opportunities
  alternatives to redundancy 30–1
  buying a franchise 205–6
  career choices 112–18
  freelance work 193–203
  interim work 204–5
  portfolio careers 206–8
  see also life choices
organizational behaviour 25–7
organizational change 72–3
outgoings 89–91
outplacement 54–5, 56–8

partners 49–50, 90–1
pay 137–9
pension arrangements 31
personal achievements 168–9
personal advisers 50–1
personal brand 121, 123
personal coaching 55–8
personal history 129–30
personal interests 111–12, 172
personal networks 145–8
personal presentation 188–9
personal profiles 153–4, 166–7
personal skills and aptitudes 119–21, 171
personal status 5–7
personality tests 110–11
portfolio careers 206–8
present-buying 101–2
psychological help 51–3
psychological response 3–5, 12–13
psychometric questionnaires 110–11

recruitment agencies 58–61
recruitment interviews 177–89
recruitment methods 58–64, 143–4
redundancy entitlement 32
redundancy notice/meeting 25–32
redundancy package 31, 93
re-employment 19
relatedness 9–10
relationships
  colleagues 9–10, 40–2
  friends and family 49–50
  support networks 65–8
research interviews 148–50
researching employers 180–1
resentment 38–9
retirement 208–9
retraining 20, 31, 159
role models 129–30

salary 137–9
saving money 89–102
selection interviews 177–89
self control 18–19
self-employment 193–203
self-knowledge 110–12
self-promotion 123–4, 150–5, 168–9
seniority 6
share options 31
sharing your feelings 14–15
shock response 4–5, 11–14
skill audit 119–20
  see also competencies
small companies 137, 200–2
social media 152–5
social support 49–50, 65–8
SPAR 184–6
spending decisions 89–102
status 5–7
storytelling 185

stress and autonomy 9
support networks 65–8
survival strategies 11–21
survivor syndrome 37–8

taking control 18–19
tax situation 32–3
temporary jobs 60, 135
therapists 51, 52–3
time management 156–7
training 20, 31, 159
transferable skills 119–20
travel 99–100
tribunals 33–5
Twitter 153, 154

uncertainty 7–8
unemployment 156, 187–8
unfair dismissal 33

vacancies 143–4
volunteering 157–8

warning signs 75, 80–1
whistleblowers 77
work experience 168–9, 170–1
work relationships 9–10, 37–8, 40–2
work-life balance 108–10, 117
worrying 8
writing a journal 17